SHIPS OF THE
MERSEY

IAN COLLARD

AMBERLEY PUBLISHING

Britannia, the first Cunarder, getting ready to depart from Liverpool on 4 July 1840. This drawing is the original artwork for a Cunard brochure of the 1920s.

First published 2008

Amberley Publishing Plc
Cirencester Road, Chalford,
Stroud, Gloucestershire, GL6 8PE

www.amberley-books.com

British Library Cataloguing in Publication Data.
A catalogue record for this book is available from the British Library.

ISBN 978 1 8468 058 6

Typesetting and Origination by diagraf**media**
Printed in Great Britain

Contents

Acknowledgements   6

Introduction   7

one   The Liners   9

two   Cargo Vessels   65

three Mersey Ferries, Coastal Vessels,

       Tugs And Dredgers   107

Lusitania in dry dock before her maiden voyage. The white flash on her side was painted out before she sailed for New York for the first time.

Introduction

In 2008 Liverpool became European Capital of Culture. The long maritime history of the city was partly responsible for the award and the fact that the city has more Grade I and II listed buildings than any other British city after London. These include the iconic 'three graces': the Royal Liver Building, the Cunard Building and the Port of Liverpool at Liverpool Pier Head. These three buildings have welcomed people arriving at Liverpool by sea for nearly one hundred years and have helped make the city a World Heritage Site, comparable to the Pyramids at Giza, Stonehenge and the Great Wall of China.

Merseyside has a proud maritime heritage as one of the most famous port cities in the world. Its multicultural mix has come from the diverse communities and nationalities that arrived by sea and contributed to the growth of the modern cosmopolitan city. The ethnic diversity of the city has been recognized and celebrated as groups were encouraged to preserve the distinctions between cultures. Almost 60,000 merchant seamen came from India to fight for Britain during the Second World War. Bengali and Chinese seamen were employed as crew on British merchant ships and many decided to settle here at the end of the war.

The earliest records mentioning the River Mersey date back to AD 1002 and Liverpool was granted borough status by Royal Charter by King John in 1207. The port developed trade routes to Ireland and the main commodity was salt, which was brought from Cheshire. There was competition with Chester in the Tudor period and trade was increased with the British colonies in the seventeenth century. It was during this period that merchants decided that they would prefer to ship goods from America through Liverpool, and it is still the major port for North Atlantic trade.

As trade increased and the strategic and economic importance of the port was recognized, new docks were built and the infrastructure increased dramatically in the eighteenth and nineteenth centuries. A board was appointed in 1857 to oversee the running and operation of the dock estate. New docks and facilities were built under the supervision and management of the Mersey Docks & Harbour Board and the port flourished and became profitable. The docks were used by all the major shipping companies of the world and most of the great ships of the twentieth century sailed into the Mersey.

Cunard, White Star, Canadian Pacific, Elder Dempster, Bibby, Henderson, Anchor and the

Pacific Steam Navigation Company and many others ran regular passenger services from the Mersey to most parts of the world. Clan, Blue Funnel, Lamport & Holt, Federal, Blue Star, Brocklebank, Harrison, Ellerman Lines and many others offered cargo- and passenger services from Liverpool and Birkenhead.

However, times were changing in the middle of the twentieth century, as the container revolution was gaining momentum and people were traveling by air rather than by passenger liner. The Mersey Docks & Harbour Company was formed in 1971 and a new dock system was built at Seaforth to accommodate the new container vessels; packaged timber, meat and bulk grain vessels and an oil terminal was developed at Tranmere in Birkenhead.

The port is now handling a similar tonnage of cargo to that of 1971 when over 14,000 workers were employed. There are now 600 people working in the port, which still maintains trading links with most major maritime centres in the world and the Port of Liverpool is still the major United Kingdom port for trade with the Eastern Seaboard of North America. A new cruise ship landing stage was opened in 2007 at the Pier Head to take advantage of the increase in the numbers and size of cruise ships operating around the British Isles. There were 3 visits by cruise vessels in 1992 and more than 30 sailings planned for 2008.

Liverpool may no longer be the home of the great passenger liners of the world or the headquarters of the main British shipping companies but it still remains as one of the major ports and maritime centres in the United Kingdom. It has survived a revolution in cargo handling and adapted its facilities to deal with a dramatic decline in passenger traffic and the recent increase in cruise ship movements. Some of the most famous ships in the world have sailed into the River Mersey and there are plans for many of the largest cruise ships to visit the river over the next few years.

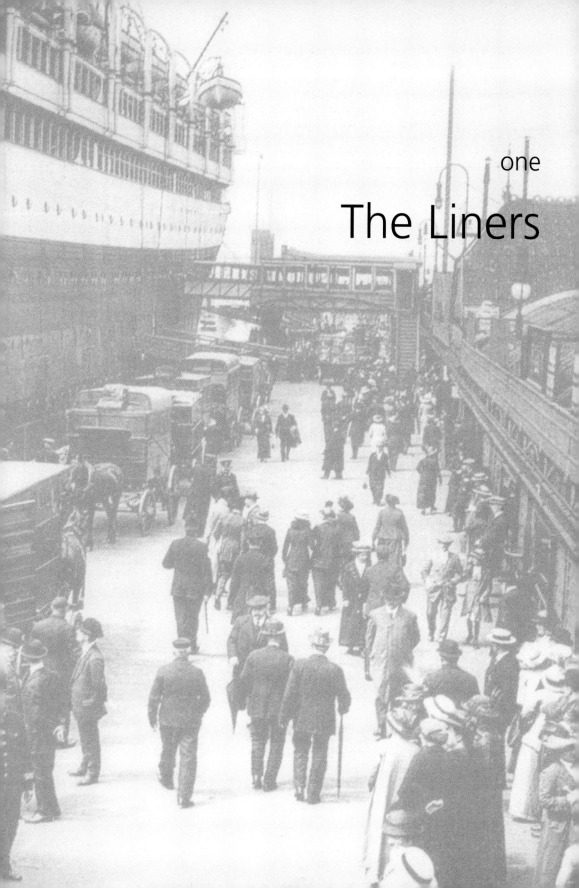

one

The Liners

Wisconsin Guion Line/Liverpool & Great Western Steamship Company (1870, 3,238grt, 112 x 13m, 11kt)
She was launched on 19 March 1870 by Palmers at Jarrow, and sailed on her maiden voyage from Liverpool to
New York via Queenstown on 6 July that year. She had accommodation for 76 first-class and 800 third-class
passengers, was operated on the same route until October 1892, and was broken up the following year.

Opposite above: Empress of England (1957, 25,585grt) prepares to sail to Canada from Liverpool Landing
Stage.

Opposite below: Gladstone Dock and Graving Dock.

Oceanic White Star Line (1899, 17,272grt, 215 x 21m, 21kt)

Oceanic was built by Harland & Wolff at Belfast and was launched on 14 January 1899. She sailed on her maiden voyage from Liverpool to New York on 6 September that year, and in September 1901 she ran down the coaster *Kincora* off Tuskar, which sank with the loss of seven of her crew. In 1905 some of the stokers in her crew refused orders and thirty-three were convicted of mutiny.

She sailed on her first voyage from Southampton to New York on 19 June 1907 and at the outbreak of the First World War she was converted to an auxiliary cruiser and was allocated to the 10th Cruiser Squadron in 1914. On 8 September that year she stranded in fog after she ran aground on the Shaalds of Foula in the Shetland Islands. The accident was attributed to a navigational error, compounded by conflicting orders given by the White Star captain and the Royal Naval captain on board. However, the courts martial exonerated both and reprimanded the navigator. *Oceanic* was declared a total loss and was broken up after the war.

Celtic, *Cedric*, *Baltic* and *Adriatic* were built by Harland & Wolff for the White Star Line's service from Liverpool to New York.

Celtic was the largest ship in the world when she was delivered in July 1901. She became an Armed Merchant Cruiser in 1914 in the 10th Cruiser Squadron, was converted to a troopship in 1916, and was struck by a torpedo in the Irish Sea in March 1917. Six people died and she was sent to Belfast to be repaired. On 8 December 1918 she took her first post-war voyage from Liverpool to New York. *Celtic* was stranded in a storm at Roches Point at the entrance to Cobh, Ireland, on 10 December 1928 and was broken up.

Cedric was completed in 1903 and also became an auxiliary cruiser in 1914 with the 10th Cruiser Squadron, and a troop and supply vessel until 1918. On 29 January 1918 she collided with the Canadian Pacific vessel *Montreal* at the Mersey Bar and *Montreal* sank. Her first post-war voyage was from Liverpool to New York on 14 December 1918 and her steerage accommodation was rebuilt for 1,000 third-class passengers in 1920. *Cedric* sailed from Liverpool to Inverkeithing on 11 January 1932 to be broken up.

Baltic was also delivered in 1904 and rescued survivors from the *Republic,* which had collided with the Italian vessel *Florida* in fog near Nantucket on 23 January 1909. *Baltic* was occasionally used as a troopship during the First World War, and in 1921 she also had her accommodation altered to take 1,000 third-class passengers. She was re-boilered in 1924 and on 6 December 1929 she saved the crew of the schooner *Northern Light* which later sank. *Baltic* was laid up in October 1932 and sailed from Liverpool to Osaka on 17 February 1933 to be broken up.

Adriatic, the last sister, was delivered in 1907 and served on both the Liverpool and Southampton to New York routes during her service with the White Star Line. On 11 August 1922 five crew died and another four were injured in an explosion in a coalbunker. She was laid up in August 1933, returned to service early in 1934, but was laid up again in September that year. Late in 1934 she was sold and arrived at Osaka on 5 March the following year to be broken up.

Above: Doric and the *Formigny* soon after their collision. A lifeboat can be seen in the foreground transferring passengers to the *Viceroy of India. Below: Doric* at Newport, Monmouthshire waiting to be broken up.

Princes Landing Stage.

Above: Carmania sinking the *Cap Trafalgar* off Trinidad Island, South America in September, 1914.

Left: Cutaway cross-section of *Carmania*.

Gennemskæring af „CARMANIA".

Caronia (1905, 19,687grt) at Liverpool Landing Stage.

Caronia and her sister, *Carmania*, were built by John Brown & Co. at Glasgow. She was launched on 13 July 1904 and was one of the largest ships built for the Cunard Line until *Lusitania* and *Mauretania*. She sailed on her maiden voyage from Liverpool to New York on 25 February 1905, and the following year she cruised from New York to the Mediterranean.

In 1914 she was sailing to Boston, but was taken over as an Armed Merchant Cruiser and fitted with 8 x 4.7 inch guns. The following year she was re-armed with 8 x 6 inch guns and she became a troop-ship in 1916. *Caronia* resumed her peacetime sailings on the Liverpool to New York route on 11 January 1919, and the following year she was converted to oil fuel, holding the distinction of being the largest ship sailing from London to New York. She was transferred to Cunard's Hamburg-Southampton-New York service in 1922, but was back on the Liverpool-New York service later that year. She was given new funnels and the passenger accommodation was remodelled at Barrow in Furness in 1924, and with the delivery of new vessels at Liverpool in 1926 she sailed out of London and cruised out of New York to Havana in the winter. She was laid up in 1931 and sold for scrapping later that year. Her sister ship, *Carmania*, was also employed on the Liverpool to New York route, and was one of the vessels involved in the rescue of survivors from the *Volturno* which was on fire in the Atlantic, when 521 out of the 654 aboard were saved.

She was converted to an Armed Merchant Cruiser in August 1914, and fitted with 8 x 4.7 inch guns. On 29 August that year she left Bermuda to patrol the area around Trinidad Island, 1,750 miles north east of Montevideo. At Trinidad Island, Hamburg-Sud Amerika's *Cap Trafalgar* had finished coaling from the *Eleonore Woermann* and was armed with two 4.1-inch guns and six heavy machine guns. Her rear funnel had been removed and she was disguised as *Carmania*. They fired at each other and *Cap Trafalgar* finally sank, but *Carmania* received twenty-nine direct hits and was on fire when the German ship sank. *Carmania* returned to commercial service in 1916, and in 1921 she was transferred to the Southampton to New York route returning to the Liverpool service the following year. In 1923 she was converted to oil burning and re-entered service on the Liverpool to Quebec route on 15 May 1924. Following service on the London-New York service in 1926, she was overhauled by Cammell Laird in 1927 and was then used for winter cruises out of New York to Havana. In 1931 she was laid up with her sister, *Caronia*, at Sheerness, and was broken up at Blyth the following year.

Above and opposite: Saxonia Cunard Line (1900, 14,281grt, 182 x 20m, 16kt)

She was built by John Brown & Co. on the Clyde and sailed on her maiden voyage on 22 May 1900 from Liverpool to Boston. In 1909 she cruised from New York to the Mediterranean, and the following year she towed *Scotia*, which had a broken shaft, 170 miles to the Azores. On 29 August 1914 she sailed from Liverpool to New York, then to Quebec to transport Canadian troops, and in 1914/15 she was used as a German prisoner-of-war ship on the Thames. In May 1915 she resumed the Liverpool-New York service, and in 1917 she carried troops from America. *Saxonia* resumed her post-war service on the London to New York route on 14 December 1918. She returned to the Liverpool-New York service in 1919 and to the London-New York route later that year. The following year she was refitted, her funnel was shortened, and she re-entered service on the London, Cherbourg or Le Havre route to New York. She was laid up at Tilbury in 1924, and was broken up the following year.

Her sister, *Ivernia*, was built by Swan, Hunter at Newcastle in 1900, and the funnels of the two sisters were the tallest ever fitted to a ship. She was intended for the Boston service, but sailed to New York from Liverpool on her maiden voyage as other ships were on Boer War contracts. In 1911 she went aground at Queenstown and was out of service for four months, taking her first Trieste-New York sailing later that year. The following summer she was again sailing from Trieste to New York, and later that year she returned to the Liverpool to Boston route. *Ivernia* became a troopship in 1914 and on 1 January 1917 she was torpedoed by the German submarine UB-47, off Cape Matapan, Greece. The destroyer HMS *Rifleman* saved over 650; others were towed to Crete in lifeboats by armed trawlers. She was carrying 2,400 Scottish troops to Alexandria, of whom 85 drowned, together with 36 crew.

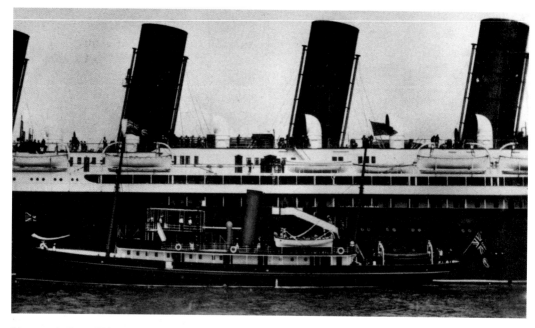

Mauretania Cunard Line (1907, 31,938grt, 241 x 27m, 25kt)

Mauretania was launched on 20 September 1906 and was built by Swan, Hunter & Wigham Richardson on the Tyne. She completed her trials on 17 September 1907, and sailed on her maiden voyage from Liverpool to Queenstown and New York on 16 November that year. On the return leg of her maiden crossing she took the record from her sister, *Lusitania*, in 4 days, 22 hours and 29 minutes, at an average speed of 23.69kt. The following year her forward derricks came loose in a January gale, breaking the bridge windows and had to be repaired with firmer stanchions.

Later that year *Lusitania* regained the record for the crossing and the following year she had new propellers fitted which created more speed with less vibration. In July she crossed in 4 days, 17 hours and 20 minutes at an average of 25.89kt. On 11 July 1913 Gladstone Dock was officially opened by King George V and Queen Mary who also visited and inspected *Mauretania*, seen above. On 5 October that year *Lusitania* became the first Cunard passenger liner to be overhauled at Gladstone Graving Dock. She took her last sailing from Liverpool to New York before war service on 10 October 1914, and then three from Halifax carrying troops. The following year she transported troops to the Dardanelles and was converted to a hospital ship with a white hull and yellow funnels. In 1916 she was laid up at Greenock and later painted in camouflage grey; during 1917-18 she carried troops from Halifax and later New York to Liverpool.

Her first post-war commercial voyage was from Liverpool to New York on 28 June 1919 and, following an extensive refit, sailed from Southampton to New York for the first time on 6 March 1920. She was damaged by fire on 25 July 1921 and converted to burn oil fuel by Swan, Hunter while she was being repaired. The Cunard Line chartered P&O's *Kaiser-i-Hind* and Canadian Pacific's *Empress of India* for several voyages before she returned to service on 25 March 1922.

She made a record crossing on 20 August 1924 and in 1930 it was decided to paint her hull white for cruising. On 26 September 1934, *Queen Mary* was launched on the Clyde, and *Mauretania* left New York on her final voyage. She was sold to Metal Industries and left Southampton on 1 July 1935 for Rosyth and her masts were shortened to allow her to pass under the Forth Railway Bridge.

*Right: Mauretani*a being broken up in 1935.

Below: Lusitania in Canada Graving Dock, Liverpool.

Left: Carinthia in the same graving dock nearly fifty years later.

Below: Empress of Britain Canadian Pacific (1906, 14,189grt, 173 x 20m, 20kt)
Empress of Britain sailed on her maiden voyage from Liverpool to Quebec on 5 May 1906 and on 27 July 1912 collided in fog with the *Helvetia* off Cape Madeleine; *Helvetia* sank. She became an auxiliary cruiser in 1914 and a troopship the following year. *Empress of Britain* was returned to Canadian Pacific in 1919 and was converted to oil burning by Fairfield's. She was renamed *Montroyal* in 1924, being placed on the Antwerp-Canada service. She was laid up off Southend in 1929 and sold for breaking up in 1930 to the Stavanger Shipbreaking Company. Her sister, *Empress of Ireland*, was also built by Fairfield's at Glasgow and delivered in 1906. On 29 May 1914 she was rammed in thick fog on the St Lawrence, near Father Point, by the Norwegian collier *Storstad*, and sank with a loss of 1,024 lives.

Olympic White Star Line (1911, 45,324grt, 269 x 28m, 22kt)

Olympic was launched on 20 October 1910 by Harland & Wolff at Belfast and sailed on her maiden voyage from Southampton to New York on 14 June 1911. In September that year she collided with the British cruiser *Hawke* off Southampton and was sent back to her builders. She was rebuilt with improved safety measures in the light of the *Titanic* disaster and was fitted with more lifeboats. In October 1914 she attempted to tow the British battleship *Audacious*, which was sinking after striking a mine in the Irish Sea. *Olympic* took the battleship's crew on board and *Audacious* sank. In 1915 she became a troopship, and on 12 May 1918 she was attacked by U-103, which ran under the bow of *Olympic* and sank. She was converted to oil-burning in 1919 and returned to the Southampton-New York service on 21 July 1920. On 16 May 1934 *Olympic* rammed the *Nantucket* lightship, which sank with the loss of seven crew. She was laid up at Southampton in 1935, sold to Metal Industries, and was broken up at Jarrow and Inverkeithing.

Titanic was also built by Harland & Wolff at Belfast, and sailed on her maiden voyage from Southampton on 10 April 1912. At 23.40hr on 14 April she collided with an iceberg, which caused a thirty-foot gash in her starboard hull and flooding five compartments. Lifeboats were launched and *Titanic* sank at 02.20hr on 15 April with the loss of 1,503 lives. *Britannic* was the third sister in the class and was also built by Harland & Wolff at Belfast. She was launched on 26 February 1914, and in November the following year the Admiralty ordered her completion as a hospital ship. She was delivered in December 1915, and on 21 November the following year she struck a mine in the Aegean, four miles west of Port St Nikolo. The watertight door system failed and water flowed into five compartments. The master tried to run the ship ashore, but an hour later the ship keeled over and sank with twenty-one fatalities.

Left and below: Aquitania Cunard Line (1914, 45,647grt, 275 x 30m, 24kt)

She was designed to operate a weekly service with *Mauretania* and *Lusitania* and, as there was no government subsidy, she was required to carry fifty per cent more passengers to be economically viable. She was ordered from John Brown & Co. on the Clyde, who needed to lengthen and strengthen the slipway to take her weight. When the Mersey Docks & Harbour Board were preparing the plans for the new Gladstone Dock, they had to amended to allow *Aquitania* to enter the new complex. She was launched on 21 April 1913, and the Clyde and the river berth had to be deepened to allow her to berth.

Aquitania sailed from Liverpool to New York on 30 May 1914 on her maiden voyage, completing only three round voyages prior to the outbreak of the First World War. She was converted to an Armed Merchant Cruiser, but was involved in an incident with her escort off Anglesey and returned to Liverpool where she was laid up. The following year she was converted to a troop transport, and carried over 30,000 service personnel to the Dardanelles. In 1916 she was painted white and became a hospital ship, carrying 25,000 injured servicemen from Turkey. She was then laid up at Liverpool in December that year, and returned to trooping duties in March 1918. She brought 60,000 United States troops to Europe and took them back home when hostilities were over.

On 19 February 1919 she took her first post-war sailing from Liverpool to New York, and later that year was converted to oil burning by Swan, Hunter & Wigham Richardson on the Tyne. She returned to service in July 1920, running with *Mauretania* and *Berengaria* which replaced *Lusitania*. In 1936 she ran in conjunction with *Queen Mary* from Southampton, and became a troopship in 1939, trooping from Sydney, Australia, to the Middle East. In 1948 she was used to repatriate United States troops, and completed twenty-five austerity voyages for the Canadian Government on the Southampton to Halifax route. She arrived at Southampton on 1 December 1949, and was sold the following year, to be broken up at Gareloch.

Vandyck Lamport & Holt Line (1921, 13,233grt, 170 x 20m, 14kt)

Vandyck was designed and built for the Liverpool-Brazil and River Plate service, and her delivery was delayed due to turbine vibration problems. She entered service on the New York-River Plate service on 27 September 1921, and made one voyage for the Royal Mail Line in 1922. In 1932 she was laid up at Southampton, and the following year was converted for cruising, her hull being painted white. She was transferred to Lamport & Holt Line in 1934, and converted to an armed boarding vessel HMS *Vandyck* in 1939. In February 1940 she sailed on one voyage to Halifax, Nova Scotia, and was then sent to Scapa Flow as an accommodation ship and later as a depot ship. She took part in the Norwegian campaign that year and was damaged by the *Admiral Hipper,* then being set on fire by German aircraft off Harstad, near Narvik, on 10 June 1940. She was abandoned, and her crew captured when they reached land. She sank the next day, following further attacks by German aircraft.

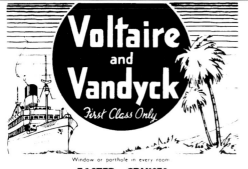

Legt and below: Vandyck's sister, *Voltaire*, sailed on her maiden voyage from Liverpool to New York on 25 November 1923 and was then based at New York. She was laid up in the River Blackwater, Essex, in 1930 and converted to a cruise liner with a white hull in 1932. She was used for trooping in 1939 and was painted grey at Southampton, also being used as an accommodation ship to HMS *Royal Oak* and HMS *Iron Duke*. When HMS *Royal Oak* was torpedoed by U-47 on 14 October, the survivors were taken on board *Voltaire*. The following day *Iron Duke* was attacked and beached, and *Voltaire* was temporarily named *Iron Duke* II. She was later converted to an Armed Merchant Cruiser becoming HMS *Voltaire*. In 1940 she was employed as a contraband and inspection vessel between Malta and Alexandria, and then became a north Atlantic escort vessel. In March 1941 she left Halifax for Trinidad and Freetown, and on 4 April she sank, following an attack by the German auxiliary cruiser *Thor*. Seventy-five crew were lost.

R.M.S. VOLTAIRE.

Above and right: Aquitania at Liverpool Landing Stage.

Above and below: Passengers and goods being loaded at Liverpool Landing Stage.

Scythia Cunard Line (1921, 19,730grt, 190 x 22m, 16kt)

Scythia was built by Vickers Armstrong at Barrow and, following her launch on 22 March 1920, she was sent to Lorient for final fitting out, because of a strike. She suffered turbine damage in 1922, and in 1928 she was used to accommodate King Amanulla and the Queen of Afghanistan at Princes Landing Stage. She also carried American tourists to Cardiff for the Welsh Eisteddfod that year.

In 1939 she completed three voyages to take United States citizens home and to evacuate children. On her return she was converted to a troopship on the Clyde. She was severely damaged at Algiers on 23 November 1942 by aerial torpedo, and sank at the berth. Temporary repairs were completed, and in January 1943 she sailed for Gibraltar and on to New York. During 1946 she brought 2,500 German prisoners of war back from Canada, and carried out trooping duties from India. In 1948 she was chartered by the International Refugee Organisation for ten voyages to carry displaced people from Germany to Canada. *Scythia* spent most of 1949 at Clydebank being overhauled by John Brown Company, and resumed service on the Liverpool to Quebec route on 17 August 1950. On 10 April 1951 she made the first Southampton-Quebec sailing for the Cunard Line since 1939. In 1957 she was chartered by the Canadian Government between Rotterdam and Quebec, later returning to the Liverpool-New York service. She left Southampton on 1 January 1958 for Inverkeithing, where she was broken up.

Scythia's sister, *Samaria*, was built by Cammell Laird at Birkenhead. When she was launched on 27 November 1920 , she was the largest ship built on Merseyside. However, her launch was delayed for six months at a cost of £250,000. Following her maiden voyage, she returned to Liverpool with engine problems, and passengers were transferred to *Laconia*. From 24 January to 22 June 1923 she took the Thomas Cook 'Round the World' cruise from New York, and repeated this cruise the following year, when she was the first Cunard to pass through the Panama Canal.

She continued to cruise from New York in 1928, and became the largest vessel to visit Galway in Ireland when she took passengers for Lourdes and Fatima. *Samaria* was converted to a troopship in 1940 and was painted grey but retained the Cunard red funnel. In 1948 she carried Canadian troops from Cuxhaven to Quebec and was sent to John Brown & Co. at Clydebank in 1950 for a major overhaul. Both sisters operated on the Liverpool and Southampton Canadian services in 1951-2 and *Scythia* went on to represent Cunard in the Coronation Naval Review at Spithead on 15 June 1953. She was laid up at Southampton in 1955 and was sold to be broken up at Inverkeithing the following year.

The Pier Head, Liverpool.

Ascania Cunard Line (1923, 14,013grt, 159 x 20m, 15kt)

Ascania was one of five Cunard 'A'- class sisters. Following her launch at Armstrong, Whitworth at Newcastle on 20 December 1923, work was suspended, and she was completed two years later for the London-Canada service. In 1928 she carried out one voyage for Anchor Line on their Glasgow-New York route.

On 3 October 1934 she went to the aid of Ropner's *Millpool*, which had sunk, and she searched the area for twenty-one hours. On 14 December she also assisted *Usworth*, which was sinking in the Atlantic. *Ascania* stood close by to enable the lifeboats to reach her. In 1938 she went aground near Quebec, and was converted to an Armed Merchant Cruiser and a landing craft infantry in 1943. On 9 July 1943 *Ascania* took part in the invasion of Sicily, and then the Anzio landings. She carried out trooping duties for the rest of the war and returned to the Liverpool-Halifax service on 20 December 1947. Two years later she was sent to Alexander Stephens on the Clyde for reconditioning, returning to the Liverpool-Quebec-Montreal service in 1950. She was called up again by the Government during the Suez Crisis in 1956, when she carried troops to Cyprus, and was broken up at Newport the following year.

Andania was built by Hawthorn Leslie & Company on the Tyne and sailed on her maiden voyage from London and Southampton to Quebec and Montreal on 1 June 1922. In 1925 she operated from Hamburg and became part of the Anchor-Donaldson sailings from Liverpool, Glasgow and Belfast to Canada. She became an Armed Merchant Cruiser in 1939, and on 16 June 1940 she was torpedoed by a German submarine, 70 miles from Reykjavik. She sank the following day.

Antonia was built by Vickers Armstrong at Barrow in 1922, and became a troopship in 1939. She carried 2,000 men to Iceland in 1940, and was later converted to an Armed Merchant Cruiser. In 1942 she was purchased by the Admiralty, converted to a Fleet Repair Ship, and renamed Wayland. She was broken up at Troon in 1948. *Ausonia* was built by Armstrong, Whitworth at Newcastle, and sailed on her maiden voyage

from Liverpool to Canada on the 31 August 1922. She was transferred to the London route the following year, and was converted to an Armed Merchant Cruiser in 1939. She was also purchased by the Admiralty, became a heavy repair ship in 1942, and was re-boilered in 1948. In 1964 she was decommissioned, and was broken up in Spain the following year.

Aurania was built by Swan, Hunter & Wigham Richardson in 1924, and the following year she also operated on the Anchor-Donaldson service from Liverpool. However, she was transferred to the London service in 1928, and was converted to an Armed Merchant Cruiser in 1939. In July 1941 she collided with an iceberg on a voyage between Iceland and Halifax. She was torpedoed in October that year, but managed to reach Scotland, where she was laid up. The following year she was also taken over by the Admiralty, and was converted to a heavy repair ship, being renamed *Artifex*. She was also re-boilered in 1948, and was broken up at La Spezia in 1961.

Alaunuia was built in 1925 by John Brown on the Clyde for the Liverpool-Montreal-Quebec service, and was transferred to the London route in 1926. She collided with the Canadian Pacific liner *Duchess of Richmond* off Quebec in November 1932. The following year she completed a programme of cruises from Liverpool to London for £4. In 1939 she became an Armed Merchant Cruiser, and was converted to a heavy repair ship for the Pacific Fleet in 1944. Later that year she was purchased by the Admiralty as a fleet repair, and later a depot ship, and was broken up at Blyth in 1957.

Sarpedon Blue Funnel Line (1923, 11,321grt, 152 x 19m, 16kt)
Launched on 2 February 1923 by Cammell Laird at Birkenhead, *Sarpedon* sailed on her maiden voyage on 9 June from Liverpool to the Far East. In 1946 she took the first post-war sailing to Australia, from Liverpool to Brisbane, and arrived at Newport, Monmouthshire, on 5 June 1953, to be broken up by John, Cashmore & Co.

Liverpool Pier Head and Landing Stage.

A White Star liner berths at Liverpool Landing Stage.

Above and next two pages: Almeda, Andalucia, Avila, Avelona and *Arandora* were the Blue Star Line 'A'-class sisters. *Almeda, Andalucia* and *Arandora* were built by Cammell Laird at Birkenhead, and *Avila* and *Avelona* by John Brown & Co. on the Clyde.

Almeda inaugurated the Blue Star passenger service from London to South America on 16 February 1927, was renamed *Almeda Star* in 1929, lengthened in 1935, and had her mainmast removed in 1937. On 22 December 1940 she was damaged during an air raid in Liverpool, and on 17 January the following year she was sunk by a torpedo from U-86 west of the Outer Hebrides. There were no survivors of the 194 passengers and 166 crew who were on board.

Andalucia entered service in March 1927, and was renamed *Andalucia Star* in 1929. She was also lengthened in 1935, and her mainmast was removed two years later. She was struck by two torpedoes from U-107 on 7 October 1942 off Freetown, on a voyage from Buenos Aires to the United Kingdom. HMS *Petunia* saved 78 out of the 83 passengers and all but two of the crew. The survivors were taken to Freetown, and sailed back to England on the *President Doumer*. Her loss meant that all five 'A'-class vessels had been sunk.

Avila was completed in 1927 for the London-La Plata service, and in 1929 she was renamed *Avila Star*, being lengthened in 1935 with accommodation for 150 first-class passengers. On 6 July 1942 she was torpedoed by U-201 off the Azores with thirty passengers and a crew of 166 on board. Another torpedo struck one of the six lifeboats, throwing the occupants into the sea. The following day the weather separated the lifeboats, and the Portuguese destroyer *Lima* rescued 110 of the survivors from three of the lifeboats, landing them in the Azores. Another lifeboat was spotted from an aircraft on 22 July, and a sloop was directed to it. The fifth lifeboat was never recovered, and seventy-three lives were lost.

Avelona was launched on 6 December 1926, and sailed on her maiden voyage from London to Madeira, Rio de Janeiro, Santos, Montevideo and Buenos Aires on 20 May the following year. She became *Avelona Star* in 1929, but because of the Depression she was converted to a cargo ship at Greenock, and all the passenger accommodation was removed in 1931. Her bridge was also moved forward by three metres. In June 1940 she

was part of a convoy sailing from Buenos Aires to the United Kingdom, and was torpedoed on 30 June by U-43, 200 miles off Cape Finisterre, and sank. The French vessel *Beignon* took the eighty survivors on board, and was later torpedoed by U-30. The destroyers *Windsor* and *Vesper* saved the 120 survivors.

Arandora was the final vessel of the class to be completed, and was launched by Cammell Laird at Birkenhead on 14 January 1927. She was converted to a cruise liner two years later by Fairfield Shipbuilding & Engineering Co. on the Clyde, and renamed *Arandora Star*. She was painted with a white hull, fitted with a swimming pool, ballroom and a parade of shops, and had accommodation for 400 passengers. On the outbreak of war in 1939 she was laid up at Falmouth, used as a test vessel for net defences against torpedoes, and converted into a troopship. On 4 June 1940 she evacuated 1,600 troops from Narvik to Glasgow, and then sailed to Brest and Quiberon to bring troops back to Britain. She returned to Bayonne, where she was under constant bomb attack, and returned to Liverpool on 29 June. On 2 July she sailed from Liverpool with 479 German and 734 Italian male internees, 86 German prisoners-of-war, 200 troops and a crew of 174. At 06.15hr on 3 June she was torpedoed by U-47, and sank within an hour. The Canadian destroyer *St Laurent* arrived at noon, and took on 868 survivors. There was a loss of life of 805 people, which included 55 of *Arandora Star's* crew and 37 military personnel.

Empress of France (1928, 20,123grt)

Built by John Brown & Co. at Clydebank, she was launched as *Duchess of Bedford* on 24 January 1928 by Mrs Stanley Baldwin, wife of the Prime Minister. *Empress of France* had been constructed for Canadian Pacific's Liverpool-Quebec and Montreal service, and was chartered to Furness, Withy, in 1933 to run with *Monarch of Bermuda*, prior to delivery of the *Queen of Bermuda*. In 1939 she was converted to a troopship and returned to the company on 2 March 1947 when she was sent to Fairfield Shipbuilding & Engineering Co., for refitting. It was planned to name her *Empress of India* but she left the Clyde as *Empress of France* for her first post-war sailing from Liverpool to Quebec and Montreal on 1 September 1948. In 1958 she had pepper-pot funnels fitted and left Liverpool on 19 December 1960 to be broken up by John Cashmore at Newport, Monmouthshire.

Above left: Empress of Japan Canadian Pacific (1930, 26,032grt, 203 x 26m, 21kt)

Built by Fairfield's on the Clyde, she sailed on her maiden voyage from Liverpool to Quebec on 14 June 1930, and after that her first voyage from Vancouver to Yokohama on 7 August. In 1939 she was converted to a troopship, and was renamed *Empress of Scotland* in 1942. She arrived back at Liverpool on 2 May 1948, and was refitted on the Clyde, sailing on her first post-war crossing from Liverpool to Greenock and Quebec on 9 May 1950. Her masts were shortened in 1952, to allow her to sail under the Quebec Bridge and up to Montreal.

She was laid up in 1957, and sold to the Hamburg Atlantic Line, sailing to Hamburg from Liverpool as *Scotland*. On arrival at Hamburg on 22 January 1958 she became *Hanseatic*. Following conversion she was placed on the Cuxhaven-Le Havre-Southampton-Cobh-New York service, and was employed on as a cruise ship the winter. On 7 September 1966 she caught fire at New York, and on 23 September she was towed to Hamburg. On arrival she was found to be beyond economic repair, and was sold to shipbreakers at Hamburg.

Above right: Empress of Britain was built on the Clyde by John Brown & Co., and was launched by Edward, Prince of Wales, on 11 June 1930. She was Canadian Pacific's largest ship and the largest ever on the Canadian service. In 1931 she completed a world cruise from New York, and was the largest ship to pass through the Suez canal. On 16 June 1935 she was in collision with *Kafiristan* in the St Lawrence, when three crew died and several were injured.

In June 1939 she carried King George VI and Queen Elizabeth from Halifax for their return sailing back to Southampton following their tour of Canada. Later that year she was converted to a troopship, and on 17 March the following year she left Southampton for Australia and New Zealand. On 12 May 1940 she left Fremantle with *Empress of Canada*, *Queen Mary*, *Aquitania*, *Mauretania* and *Andes*. On 26 October, off the West Coast of Ireland, she was attacked by a German Focke-Wulf Condor aircraft and set on fire. The blaze was so intense that the order was given to abandon ship and she was taken in tow by the Polish destroyer *Burza* and the tugs *Marauder* and *Thames*. However, her position became known by the German submarine U-32, who followed her and torpedoed her twice on 28 October, sinking her with a loss of forty-five lives. U-32 was sunk by the destroyer *Harvester* two days later, but *Empress of Britain* was the largest liner sunk during the Second World War.

Georgic (1932, 27,759grt) leaves Princes Landing Stage on her maiden voyage.

She was built by Harland & Wolff at Belfast and launched on 12 November 1931. Georgic sailed on her maiden voyage to New York on 25 June 1932, and was transferred to the London-New York service in 1935. She returned to the Liverpool service in 1939, and was fitted out as a troopship on the Clyde in March 1940.

On 14 July 1941 she was badly damaged off Port Tewfik during a German air raid, when she caught fire. With eighteen feet of water in her engine room, her captain beached her. The salvage operation took two months to re-float her, and she was towed to Port Sudan by the cargo vessels *Clan Campbell* and *City of Sydney*, and then to Karachi and Bombay where temporary repairs were carried out. She left Bombay on 20 January 1943, and arrived back at Liverpool on 1 March. Work was carried out by Harland & Wolff, which involved removing her fore-funnel and mainmast, and she was sold to the Ministry of War and managed by the Cunard-White Star Line. *Georgic* returned to service in December 1944, and repatriated former prisoners of war from the Far East.

In 1948 *Georgic* was sent to the Tyne to be converted to a one-class emigrant ship, and sailed on her first voyage from Liverpool to Sydney on 11 January 1949. The following year she returned to service, and sailed on her first post-war voyage from Liverpool to New York on 4 May. In April 1953 she was advertised for sale, but was reprieved and placed on Australian migrant service. In 1955 she carried troops from Australia to Kuala Lumpur, and also carried French *legionnaires* to Algiers. Later that year she was sold to Shipbreaking Industries, and arrived at Faslane on 1 February 1956 to be broken up.

Britannic (1930, 26,943grt) in Huskisson Dock, Liverpool in 1958.

Built by Harland & Wolff at Belfast, she was launched on 6 August 1929, and sailed on her maiden voyage from Liverpool to New York on 28 June 1930. *Britannic* was transferred to the London-New York route in 1935, and became a troopship in August 1939. She returned to Cunard in March 1947, and was refitted at Liverpool with accommodation for 429 first-class and 564 tourist-class passengers. She left Liverpool on 22 May 1948 on her first post-war crossing to New York.

By 1960 she had completed 275 peacetime and wartime crossings, travelling over 2,000,000 miles and carrying over 1,200,000 passengers on her North Atlantic crossings and cruises. She arrived in Liverpool from New York on 4 December that year, at the end of her final Atlantic crossing, and was sold at Inverkeithing, where she arrived on 19 December to be broken up.

Britannic leaving Gladstone Dock (above) and berthing at Liverpool Landing Stage (below).

Above, left and right: Queen of Bermuda Furness Withy (1933, 22,575grt, 176 x 23m, 21kt)
Built by Vickers Armstrong Ltd at Barrow, she arrived on the Mersey on 10 February 1933 for dry-docking and hull cleaning prior to her trials on 14 February. She and her sister ship, *Monarch of Bermuda*, were built for the line's New York-Bermuda service, and she sailed on her maiden voyage from Liverpool to New York on 21 February. In 1939 she was converted to an Armed Merchant Cruiser and fitted with 7 x 6 inch guns and anti-aircraft weapons. Her third funnel was removed, and she saw service in the South Atlantic. In 1943 she was converted to a troopship, and carried over 97,000 troops in this role.

Queen of Bermuda was refitted in 1947, her third funnel was replaced, and her original eight boilers were replaced by three. She returned to the Bermuda service on 12 February 1949, and, in her 1961/62 winter overhaul, she was rebuilt with one funnel. She continued in service until 1966, when she was broken up at Faslane.

Her sister, *Monarch of Bermuda*, was completed in 1933 for the New York to Bermuda service. At the outbreak of the Second World War she was laid up at New York, and in October 1939 she sailed to Liverpool and was converted to a troopship. In 1940 she took Italian diplomats to Lisbon for exchange with their British counterparts, and carried 2,000 troops in the Norwegian campaign. In July that year she carried Britain's £40 million gold reserves from Greenock to Halifax. She was converted to a landing ship infantry, in 1942 and carried troops to North Africa, Oran and Sicily.

On 24 March 1947 she was virtually destroyed by fire during conversion back into a passenger ship. She was bought by the Ministry of Transport and rebuilt at Southampton as an emigrant ship for Australia, managed by Shaw Savill & Albion. In 1953 she carried out trooping duties to Korea. She was sold to the Greek Line in 1958, renamed *Arkadia*, and sailed on her first voyage from Bremerhaven to Quebec and Montreal. *Arkadia* arrived at Valencia to be broken up on 18 December 1966.

Circassia Anchor Line (1937, 11,136grt, 154m x 20m, 17kt)

Caledonia, *Cilicia*, and *Circassia* were built by Fairfield's on the Clyde for the Anchor Line service from Glasgow, then Liverpool to Bombay. *Circassia* sailed on her maiden voyage from Glasgow and Liverpool to Bombay on 14 October 1937. She became an Armed Merchant Cruiser in 1940, a troopship in 1942, and was rebuilt as a large landing-ship infantry in 1943. She resumed service for her owners on 21 August 1947, and made Anchor Line's final sailing between Glasgow, Liverpool and Bombay on 13 January 1966. She was broken up at Alicante later that year.

   Cilicia entered service in 1938, and became an Armed Merchant Cruiser in 1939. She was the 'task-ship' for the establishment of a meteorological station on Tristan da Cunha in 1943, and in 1944 she was converted to a troopship at Mobile, USA, carrying 2,400 troops to Port Said. She returned to Anchor Line in 1946, after carrying over 16,000 troops and prisoners of war. She re-entered service in 1947, and was sold in 1967 and used as a floating hostel for training stevedores, based in Parkhaven, Holland, renamed *Jan Backx*. In 1980 she was towed by the Smit tug *Zwarte Zee* to Bilbao to be broken up. *Caledonia* was built after the War in 1948, and completed her service with Anchor Line in 1965, when she became a floating hostel for students of Amsterdam University. She was broken up in Hamburg in 1970.

Mauretania Cunard Line (1939, 35,739grt, 235m x 27m, 23kt)

Her keel was laid on 24 May 1937, and she became the first liner for Cunard-White Star Limited and the largest passenger liner to be built in England. *Mauretania* was built without any government subsidy, and was designed to relieve the *Queen Mary* when required. She was launched by Cammell Laird at Birkenhead on 28 July 1938 and sailed on her trials the following March, achieving an average speed of 22kt. *Mauretania* sailed on her maiden voyage from Liverpool on 17 June 1939, when large crowds on both sides of the Mersey saw her sail to New York. She was transferred to the London-New York route, and became the largest vessel to use the King George V dock. She sailed from Southampton to New York on the 14 September, returning to Liverpool, and after another round trip she sailed to New York where she was laid up on 16 December that year.

Mauretania became a troopship in March, 1940 and sailed from New York to Sydney via the Panama Canal and Honolulu for conversion. She sailed from Sydney to the Clyde on 5 May with over 2,000 troops and over the course of the Second World War made forty-eight trooping voyages covering 540,000 miles and carrying over 350,000 troops. On 2 August 1946 she arrived back at Liverpool to be converted back to a passenger liner at Gladstone Dock by Cammell Laird. She left Liverpool on a short two-and-a-half day cruise on 18 April the following year but because of bad weather the cruise lasted five days. She made her first post-war sailing from Liverpool to New York on 26 April and was later transferred to Southampton.

She was fitted with air-conditioning during an overhaul in 1957 enabling her to undertake a cruise programme that included round-the-world voyages. She was painted in "*Caronia*" green in 1962 and the following year she was placed on the New York-Cannes-Genoa-Naples service. Her final sailing on this route was on 15 September 1965 thereafter returning to Southampton where she was sold. *Mauretania* arrived at Inverkeithing on 23 November to be broken up by Thos. W. Ward.

Above: Devonia (1939, 11,275grt) at Princes Landing Stage in 1964.

She was built by the Fairfield Shipbuilding & Engineering Co. on the Clyde as a troopship for the Bibby Line of Liverpool under the name *Devonshire*. In the Second World War she completed trooping duties the Mediterranean, the Far East and around Africa. On 7 June 1944, during the invasion of Europe, *Devonshire* and three other Bibby Line ships, *Cheshire, Lancashire* and *Worcestershire,* sailed in line in the English Channel carrying 10,000 troops to the Normandy bridgeheads. *Devonshire* was refitted in 1953 and returned to trooping duties the following year. She was sold to British India in 1962 and converted to an educational cruise ship by Barclay Curle on the Clyde and became *Devonia*. She was broken up at La Spezia in 1967.

Left: The South Docks system at Liverpool.

Right and below: Media Cunard Line (1947, 13,345grt, 162 x 21m, 17kt)

Media was built by John Brown & Co. at Clydebank and her sister, *Parthia,* was delivered to the Cunard Line by Harland & Wolff at Belfast. Both vessels were designed as cargo-passenger vessels and had accommodation for 250 first-class passengers. *Media* was the first post-war building for the company and sailed on her maiden voyage on 20 August 1947, from Liverpool to New York. In the winter of 1952-3 both vessels were fitted with stabilizers and in 1961 she was trapped in Gladstone Graving Dock for months due to a strike by the Amalgamated Engineering Union members. Both sisters were placed on the market and *Media* was sold to Compagnia Genovese di Armamaento, Genoa, in 1961 and became *Flavia.* She sailed on the Genoa-Suez-Australia and Bremerhaven-Southampton-Australia routes and in 1968 she was cruising in the Mediterranean and Caribbean. The following year she was sold to Costa Line of Naples and cruised out of Miami until 1982 when she became *Flavian* and was laid up at Hong Kong. In 1986 she was sold to Lavia Shipping S.A., Panama, renamed *Lavia* and continued to be laid up at Hong Kong. However, on 7 January 1989 she was damaged by a serious fire and was beached and declared a total loss.

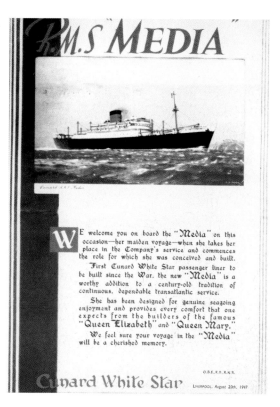

R.M.S "MEDIA"

WE welcome you on board the "Media" on this occasion—her maiden voyage—when she takes her place in the Company's service and commences the role for which she was conceived and built.

First Cunard White Star passenger liner to be built since the War, the new "Media" is a worthy addition to a century-old tradition of continuous, dependable transatlantic service.

She has been designed for genuine seagoing enjoyment and provides every comfort that one expects from the builders of the famous "Queen Elizabeth" and "Queen Mary."

We feel sure your voyage in the "Media" will be a cherished memory.

O.B.E.,R.D.,R.N.R.

Cunard White Star

LIVERPOOL, August 22th, 1947.

Above: Media's sister, *Parthia*, was sold to the New Zealand Shipping Company in 1962 becoming *Remuera* and transferred to the Eastern & Australian S.S.Co. in 1965 and renamed *Aramac* for their Melbourne-Hong Kong-Japan route. She was broken up at Kaohsiung where she arrived on 22 November 1969.

Left: Nova Scotia Johnson Warren Lines Ltd. (1947, 7,438grt, 134m x 19m, 15kt). She and her sister ship *Newfoundland* were built by Vickers Armstrong at Newcastle for the service to Canadian ports. *Nova Scotia* sailed on her maiden voyage from Liverpool to St Johns, Newfoundland-Halifax-Boston on 2 September 1947, and they operated as Furness Warren Line. Their passenger capacity was reduced to 12 in 1962 and *Nova Scotia* was sold to H.C. Sleigh Ltd, Melbourne, that year and renamed *Francis Drake* for the Hong Kong-China-Japan monthly service. *Newfoundland* was also sold to the same line in 1962 and became *George Anson*. Both vessels were broken up at Kaohsiung in 1971.

Caronia Cunard Line (1949, 34,274grt, 218m x 28m, 22kt)

Caronia was built as a dual-purpose vessel used as a cruise ship and also on the North Atlantic. She was built by John Brown & Co. at Glasgow on the same berth as *Caronia* (1) and was launched on 30 October 1947. She sailed on her maiden voyage from Southampton to New York on 4 January 1949 and was painted green for the whole of her career and in her winter overhaul in 1956 she was fitted with air-conditioning. On 14 April 1958 the lines from her tugs parted and she demolished a lighthouse and buckled her bow whilst entering Yokohama Harbour.

In 1962 she was the first Cunard liner to visit Varna on the Black Sea since the Crimean War and was laid up at Southampton in November, 1967. The following year she was sold to Universal Line S.A., became *Columbia* and sailed from Southampton to Piraeus for overhaul, emerging as *Caribia*. On 11 March 1969 she suffered a serious engine room explosion off St Thomas and one crewman was killed. She drifted for twenty hours and was towed into New York on 25 March and laid up at Gravesend Bay. She left New York on 27 April 1974 in tow of the tug *Hamburg* to be broken up at Taiwan. When the ship was near Apra Harbour, Guam, the generator on the tug failed and *Caribia* was cut adrift and was driven aground on the Apra breakwater where she broke into three pieces and was later demolished.

Franconia Cunard Line (1955, 22637grt., 185m x 29m, 20kt)

Franconia was built as *Ivernia* and was the second vessel delivered by John Brown & Co. of the *Saxonia* Class. *Saxonia, Ivernia, Carinthia* and *Sylvania* were all delivered for Cunard's Canadian Services, although *Sylvania* later replaced *Britannic* on the Liverpool-New York service. *Ivernia's* maiden voyage on 1 July 1955 from Greenock to Quebec and Montreal was delayed because of a catering strike and she then operated from Liverpool. However, she was transferred to Southampton in 1957 and went aground in Southampton Water on 22 April 1961 and required nine tugs to re-float her after five hours.

In 1962 she was sent to her builders together with *Saxonia* to be rebuilt and she was renamed *Franconia*, painted green and employed cruising out of New York in summer and Port Everglades in the winter. In November, 1967 she became the last Cunard liner to terminate a scheduled sailing in Liverpool and the following year she ran from New York to Bermuda for the Furness-Bermuda Line and he hull was painted white.

The four Canadian sisters were put up for sale in 1971 and *Franconia* was laid up at Southampton and was berthed on the River Fal with *Carmania* the following year. She was sold to Russian interests in August 1973, became *Fedor Shalyapin*. She sailed on her first voyage from Southampton to Sydney, and Auckland on 20 November that year. She was renamed *Salona* for the delivery voyage to the breakers at Alang where she arrived on 6 February 2004.

Opposite above: Main First Class Lounge on *Caronia*.

Opposite below: Cinema Theatre, First and Cabin Class on *Caronia*.

Above: Carmania Cunard Line (1954, 22592grt, 185 x 29m, 20kt)

Launched as *Saxonia* by Lady Churchill on 17 February 1954, she sailed on her maiden voyage from Liverpool to Quebec and Montreal on 2 September that year. She was moved to the Southampton service in 1957 and to the London-New York route in 1961. Together with *Ivernia* she was converted to dual North Atlantic and cruising service, painted green and renamed *Carmania*. From 1964 to 1970 she was used on Mediterranean fly-cruises and given a white hull.

In January 1969 she was aground for five days at Newport News and did not return to service until 8 May and from 1970 her port of registry became Southampton. She was laid up in 1971 and moved to the River Fal the following year. In 1973 she was sold to Nikreis Maritime Corporation and renamed *Leonid Sobinov*, managed by CTC Lines for both the Southampton-Australia and New Zealand service and cruises. In 1999 when she was delivered to Indian shipbreakers at Alang on 1 October and had been anchored off Alang since 1 April that year.

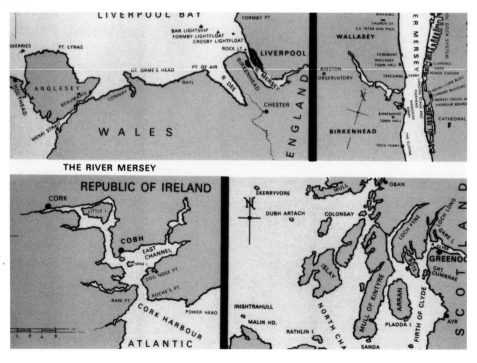

Opposite below: Cunard Line map of the approaches to Liverpool, Cork and the Clyde.

Above: Carinthia at Princes Landing Stage in 1962.

She was launched on 14 December 1955 by Princess Margaret at John Brown's yard on the Clyde and sailed on her maiden voyage from Liverpool to Quebec and Montreal on 27 June 1956. The only one of the four Canadian sisters not to be given a white hull, she made the last Cunard passenger sailing from Liverpool to Montreal on 13 October 1967. On her return she was laid up at Southampton and sold to the Sitmar Line in 1968 and renamed *Fairland*. She sailed to Trieste in January 1970 for conversion by Arsenale Triestino and was renamed *Fairsea* in 1971, for the Australian service. The following year she was cruising out of Fort Lauderdale and Miami and in 1983 she moved to the West Coast of America, cruising out of San Francisco.

In July 1988 the Sitmar Line was acquired by P&O and *Fairsea* became *Fair Princess*. In 2000 she became *China Seas Discovery* owned by Emerald Cruises. She was laid up at Kaohsiung in 2002. The following year it was announced that she would be based at Keelung, providing one-night gambling trips for four nights a week and also three-night cruises to Naha and Ishigaki in Japan. She was renamed *Sea Discovery* in 2005 and arrived at Alang to be broken up on 18 November that year.

Above: The royal car awaits Her Majesty Queen Elizabeth the Queen Mother outside Woodside Station, Birkenhead, when she arrived by royal train to launch the Union Castle Line vessel *Windsor Castle* on 23 June 1959.

Opposite below: Reina del Mar (1956, 20,750grt) leaves Princes Landing Stage on a cruise in 1963. She was built by Harland & Wolff at Belfast for the Pacific Steam Navigation Company's passenger and cargo service to South Americ. She sailed on her maiden voyage from Liverpool to Valparaiso, via the Panama Canal on 3 May 1956.

In 1963 she was chartered to the Travel Savings Association and was converted by Harland & Wolff at Belfast, the following year. She was placed under the Union Castle management and painted in their colours. Her first cruise was on 10 June 1964 from Southampton to New York and in 1969 she was transferred to Royal Mail ownership being purchased by the Union Castle Line in 1973. *Reina del Mar* was broken up by Tung Cheng Steel Manufacturing Co. at Kaohsiung where she arrived on 30 July 1975.

Above: Oxfordshire (1957, 20,586grt) berthed astern of the Isle of Man Steam Packet vessel *King Orry* (1946, 2,485grt) at Princes Landing Stage in 1957 *Oxfordshire* was built as a troop transport, managed by the Bibby Line. She entered service in 1957 on a twenty-year charter to the Ministry of Transport and used Liverpool as her home port until May 1958, when she moved to Southampton. Her trooping duties finished in 1962 when the Government ended the contract and *Oxfordshire* was laid up on the River Fal. She was bought by the Fairline Shipping Corporation in 1963 and was sent to Wilton-Fijenoord N.V., Schiedam to be converted to a passenger and cruise liner. She was then bought by the Sitmar Line during the conversion and was completed by Harland & Wolff at Southampton under the name *Fairstar*. Her first sailing was on 19 May 1964 from Southampton to Brisbane. She arrived at Alang on 11 April 1997 to be broken up.

In 1988 Sitmar were taken over by P&O. In June 1991 she broke down with generator failure and was towed into Vung Tau while cruising out of Singapore.

Promenade Deck on *Empress of England* (1956, 25585grt).

Above and below: Empress of England (1957, 25,585grt) at Princes Landing Stage in 1963.
Launched by Prime Minister's wife, Lady Eden, at Vickers Armstrong Ltd. in Walker on Tyne. She sailed on her maiden voyage from Liverpool to Quebec and Montreal on 18 April 1957 and was chartered to the Travel Savings Association in 1963 returning to Canadian Pacific service in April 1965.

In 1970 she was sold to Shaw, Savill & Albion and took one sailing from Liverpool and Southampton to Sydney before returning to Cammell Laird where she was delayed by strikes at the yard. She finally left Birkenhead on 17 September 1971 six months late, and twelve summer cruises were cancelled. She sailed on a single Southampton-Mediterranean cruise on 16 October and left on her sailing to Auckland on 5 November. In 1973 she was cruising out of Sydney but she was experiencing engine breakdowns. She returned to Britain, being withdrawn from service in 1975 and broken up at Kaohsiung where she arrived on 17 July that year.

Above: The Blue Funnel Line cargo and passenger liner *Centaur* (1964, 8,262grt) berthing at Princes Landing Stage in 1964. She was built by John Brown & Co. on the Clyde and designed for the three-weekly service between Fremantle, Western Australian ports and Singapore and was launched by Mrs Brand, wife of the Prime Minister of Western Australia on 30 June 1963. *Centaur* sailed on her maiden voyage from Liverpool on 20 January 1964 to Sydney and her first voyage from Australian ports was on charter to the Australian Chambers of Trade. Her final departure from Fremantle was on 15 September 1981 and the following year she was chartered to St Helena Shipping to replace St Helena, which was sent to the Falklands. The charter was completed in 1983 when *St Helena* returned to service. *Centaur* was sold to Shanghai Hai Xing Shipping Company in 1985 and renamed *Hai Long, Hai Da* in 1986, being broken up in China in 2006.

Opposite above: The Swedish-America Line passenger liner *Kungsholm* (1965, 26,678grt) at Princes Landing Stage.
Kungsholm was built by John Brown & Co. on the Clyde and was launched on 14 April 1965, sailing on her maiden voyage from Gothenburg to New York on 22 April the following year. She was used by the company mainly for cruising and was sold to Flagship Cruises, Monrovia, in 1975 when she was used for cruising out of New York. She was sold to P&O in 1979 becoming *Sea Princess*, operated by the *Princess* Cruise Division. She was renamed *Victoria* in 1995, *Mona Lisa* in 2003, *Oceanic II* in 2007, and *Mona Lisa* in 2008.

Opposite below: Southern Cross Shaw Savill Line (1955, 20,203grt, 184 x 24m, 20kt)
Southern Cross was the first British liner to have her funnel aft of the passenger decks. She was built by Harland & Wolff at Belfast and was designed for Shaw Savill's round-the-world service sailing on her maiden voyage from Southampton on 29 March 1955. In 1971 she carried out a number of cruises from Liverpool and was laid up at Southampton later that year. In 1972 she moved to the River Fal and was sold to Cia de Vap Cerulea S.A. the following year renamed *Calypso* and refitted at Piraeus as a cruise liner. She became *Azure Seas* in 1980, *Ocean Breeze* in 1991 and was broken up at Chittagong in 2003.

Her sister, *Northern Star* (1962, 2,4731grt), was less successful than *Southern Cross*. She sailed on her maiden voyage on 10 July 1962 after calling at Liverpool on her delivery cruise from her builders, Vickers Armstrong on the Tyne. When Shaw Savill decided to end the round-the-world service, *Northern Star* operated a number of cruises and it was decided that she should be sold. She arrived at Kaohsiung on 11 December 1975 to be broken up.

Left: Swimming Pool on *Southern Cross*.

Opposite below: Windsor Castle (1960, 37,640grt) was built by Cammell Laird at Birkenhead and was dry-docked at Gladstone Graving Dock prior to her trials in 1960. She was the largest liner built in England at the time and the first built at Birkenhead. Her maiden voyage was on 18 August 1960, when she sailed from Southampton to Cape Town and Durban carrying 191 first-class and 591 tourist-class passengers and 475 crew. She was designed with extensive cargo spaces, which were carried in seven holds for general and also refrigerated cargoes.

Windsor Castle remained on the mailship service from Southampton to South Africa until 1977 when she made her last passenger sailing on 12 August. She was sold to John Latsis at Piraeus and sailed from Southampton to Greece on 3 October. Renamed *Margarita L* she was refitted as an 852-berth luxury accommodation ship and was initially used as an office and leisure centre for the Latsis-owned Petrola International S.A. Construction Company at Rabegh. However, in 1979 she replaced the ex-Elder Dempster Liner *Aureol* which was renamed *Marianna VI*, at a special jetty two miles north of Jeddah, Saudi Arabia, at the centre of a complex of car parks, swimming pools and sports facilities.

She returned to Greece for overhaul in 1983 and was towed to Eleusis Bay in 1990 where she was laid up with occasional private use by Mr Latsis and offered for sale in 1998. She became *Rita* in 2005 and was broken up at Alang that year.

Above: Dunera (1937, 11,197grt) in the Mersey at the end of an educational cruise in 1965. *Dunera* was built as a troopship and was employed in the Middle East, South Africa, Singapore and Australia, between 1939 and 1941. The following year she was converted to a landing ship. In September that year she was at the Majunga landing and in July 1943 she was at the Sicily assaults. In August 1944 *Dunera* was the Headquarters ship of the 7th US Army for the South of France invasion and the following May she took part in the re-occupation of Rangoon. She was the lead ship at the Malaya landings and then-completed trooping duties between India and Malaya. In 1945 she carried troops from India to Japan. She was at her builders on the Clyde, between March 1950 and May the following year being rebuilt to be employed to carry troops to Cyprus, Ceylon and Malaya.

In 1961 she was converted to an educational cruise ship by Vickers Armstrong at Hebburn on the Tyne, with accommodation for 194 cabin-class passengers and 834 students. Her first cruise was from Greenock with 732 students on 12 April 1961. *Dunera* was broken up at Bilbao in 1967.

Uganda British India Line (1952, 14,430grt, 165 x 22m, 18kt)

Uganda was also employed as an educational cruise ship from Liverpool. She was built for the British India Line's London-East Africa service and operated this route with her sister *Kenya* until 1967 when the service was closed. She left London on 4 March that year to be converted to an educational cruise ship by Howaldtswerke at Hamburg. Her first cruise was from Southampton but she became Mediterranean-based and she was overhauled each year at Malta.

On 10 April 1982 she was requisitioned to be converted to a hospital ship for the Falklands conflict. She was at Alexandria and passengers were taken to Naples and Gibraltar. She was given a helicopter deck and her dormitories were converted to wards staffed by twelve doctors, 124 medical staff and nurses. She left Gibraltar on 19 April for the Falklands. In service she was the 'mother ship' for the hydrographic vessels *Hecla*, *Herald* and *Hydra* who acted as ambulance ships. Argentina surrendered on 14 June and *Uganda* was re-registered as a hospital ship the following month. She was sent to Smith's Shiprepairers at North Shields to be converted back to her educational role and sailed on her first cruise on 18 September.

In 1983 she was chartered by the Ministry of Defence to carry troops between Ascension Island and Port Stanley and arrived back at Falmouth on 25 April 1985 when the charter ended. She was sold to Triton Shipping Co., London, renamed *Triton* and left the Fal on 20 May 1986 to be broken up at Kaohsiung. However, following arrival she was blown ashore by cyclone 'Wayne' and turned on her side. The photograph shows her leaving the River Fal anchorage on 20 May 1986.

Monte Anaga Aznar Line (1959, 6,813grt, 131 x 18m, 14kt)
She operated with her sisters *Monte Umbe* (1959, 9,971grt), *Monte Urquiola* (1949, 7,723grt) and
Monte Arucas (1956, 4,691grt) on Anzar Line's service from Liverpool to the Canary Islands. *Monte
Anaga* was sold to the Government of Mexico in 1975 to be used as a training ship when she was
renamed *Primero De Junio*.

Swimming pool on Fyffes Line *Golfito* (1949, 8,740grt).

Above and below: Queen Elizabeth 2 (1969, 67,140grt) on her first visit to the Mersey on 24 July 1990.

two

Cargo Vessels

Above: Mahronda Brocklebank Line (1925 7,880grt, 143 x 20m, 14kt)
She was built by William Hamilton & Co. Ltd at Port Glasgow for the Brocklebank Line's service from Calcutta to the United States and back to the United Kingdom. On 11 June 1942, she was torpedoed and sunk by a Japanese submarine off Mozambique on a voyage from Liverpool to Karachi.

Opposite above: Malakand Brocklebank Line (1919, 7,649grt, 143 x 20m, 14kt)
This is one of Brocklebank's most famous ships on Merseyside because of the events of the night of 3/4 May 1941 when Liverpool suffered one of its worst air raids. *Malakand* was berthed at No.2 Huskisson Dock with a cargo of ammunition, incendiary and high explosive bombs. There were reports that over 500 German planes were bombing Liverpool that night and the people of the Wirral said that it looked as if the whole of Liverpool city centre was on fire. A deflated barrage balloon slipped from its mooring and then became tangled with the ships rigging. It then fell on the deck and burst into flames. A shower of incendiaries had ignited some of the sheds and the flames quickly enveloped *Malakand*. The crew even attempted to scuttle the vessel and the captain gave the instruction to abandon ship but the vessel exploded, causing extensive damage to the whole of the Huskisson dock system.

Opposite below: Wayfarer Harrison Line (1925, 5,068grt, 120 x 16m, 12kt).
Launched on 4 June 1925 by Chas Connell & Co., Glasgow as a continuation of the 'Dramatist' class. On 14 April 1944 she was loading at Bombay, when the *Fort Stikine*, loaded with 1,300 tons of TNT, blew up, and nineteen other merchant vessels and three Indian warships were lost. The disaster also caused severe starvation problems in the area as over 40,000 tons of food was destroyed and 900 people completely disappeared. *Wayfarer* survived the explosion but was torpedoed by U-862 east of Mozambique on 19 August that year. Ten crew survived on a raft and later landed in Mozambique.

Above: Dalesman Harrison Line (1940, 6,348grt, 140 x 17m, 13kt)

Delivered in July 1940, she achieved 17kt on trials although her design speed was 13kt. On 14 May 1941 she was sunk during a German air attack at Suda Bay, Crete. Thirty-two of her crew were taken prisoner and twenty-four escaped to Egypt on an abandoned tank landing craft. Captain J.H. Dobson was awarded the MBE for taking his men to safety. The vessel was raised and renamed *Pluto* later that year, but was damaged at Trieste by Allied bombers in 1944. Later that year she was recovered when Trieste was captured, being repaired and renamed *Empire Wily* by the Ministry of War Transport. In November 1946, she was returned to Harrison Line and renamed *Dalesman* being owned by them until 1959, when she was broken up by Van Heyghen at Ghent.

Opposite below: Pacific Exporter Furness Withy (1928, 6,722grt, 133 x 18m)
Delivered to the Norfolk & North American Line, she was damaged in an air raid on Manchester Docks on 23 December 1940. She was sold in 1951 and renamed *Giacomo C* after the founder of Gianomo Costa of Genoa, and broken up at Savona in 1958. *Pacific Exporter* was part of a class of four similar vessels. *Pacific Enterprise* was on a voyage from Vancouver to Manchester on 8 September 1949 and grounded in fog on Wash Rock at Point Arena, California, when she was abandoned. *Pacific Reliance* was torpedoed by U-29 on 4 March 1940 in the Irish Sea on a voyage to Liverpool and London and sank. *Pacific Pioneer* was torpedoed by U-132 in the Atlantic on 29 July 1942.

Above: Onistsha Elder Dempster 1952 5802grt. 137m x 18m 11kt
Launched by Harland & Wolff at Belfast on the 29 January 1952 to replace the *Mary Kingsley*. She was sold to Cisne Cia.de Nav. S.A., Piraeus in 1972 and renamed Amvourgon. On 8 January 1975 on a voyage from Quebec to Baltimore she suffered an engine room fire and was abandoned off Cape Gaspe. She was taken in tow three days later and was condemned as beyond repair at Halifax where she left, in tow, on 7 May to be broken up at Santander.

Matru Guinea Gulf Line (1947, 4,811grt, 124 x 17m, 12kt)
Built by the Furness Shipbuilding Company at Haverton Hill-on-Tees as *Sherbro* for the Elder Dempster Line. She was transferred to the Guinea Gulf Line in 1965 becoming *Matru*. Two years later she was sold to Agia Eftichia Shipping of Famagusta and renamed *Agia Eftichia*, becoming *Moka* for the Inchop Shipping Corporation, Somalia in 1971. She was sold for breaking up at Gadani Beach later that year.

Advertisement for Elder Dempster's West Africa service.

A locomotive being loaded onto a vessel in the West Float, Birkenhead.

Advertisement for Harland & Wolff, Liverpool.

Lamport and Holt Line

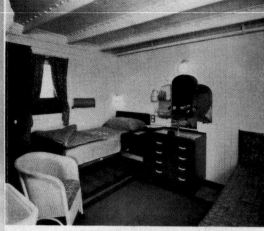

SINGLE CABIN

PASSENGER SAILINGS

BRAZIL
URUGUAY
ARGENTINA

DINING SALOON
leading into Lounge

Above and opposite above: Rubens Lamport & Holt Line (1952, 4,459grt, 133 x 17m, 12kt)
Completed in October 1952 as *Siddons*, she became *Rubens* in 1955. In 1965 she was transferred to the Booth Line, renamed *Bernard*. She reverted back to Lamport & Holt ownership in 1967, becoming *Rossini*. She reverted to *Bernard* in 1970, before being chartered to Sopac Bulk Carriers in 1973 and renamed *Berwell Adventure*. She became *Al Turab* in 1975 and arrived at Gadani Beach to be broken up in December 1977.

Opposite below: Boniface (1979, 3,636grt) and *Benedict* (1979, 3,636grt) laid up in Vittoria Dock, Birkenhead.
They were both built at Engenharie e Maquinas S.A. at Rio de Janeiro and *Boniface* left Heysham, on Booth Line's final ship owning voyage to Belem, on 24 April 1986. On her return she was laid up at Birkenhead with her sister, *Benedict* and both were sold to Losinjska Plovidba OOUR Brodarstvo, Rijeka, Coatia, in November 1986. *Benedict* became *Zamet* and *Boniface* was renamed *Pecine*. They were owned by Cool Wind Navigation Corporation in 1990. *Zamet* was renamed *Ismail Prince* in 2005 and *Pecine* became *Seven Star* in 2005 and *Reef Mahr* in 2006.

Above: Bordazuri (1947, 5,947grt) was built by Doxford at Pallion as *Eastbank* for the Bank Line. She became *Bordazuri* in 1965, *Pella* in 1972, *Sierra* in 1974 and *Makedonia II* in 1977. On 14 November 1977 she suffered a serious engine failure in the South Adriatic and was broken up at La Spezia in 1980.

Left: Langton Dock Entrance.

Opposite above: Caledonia Star Blue Star Line (1942, 9,205grt, 149 x 19m, 11kt)
She was launched on 29 July 1942 as *Empire Wisdom* for the Ministry of War Transport with Clan Line as managers. She was completed in November 1942 with a thin wartime funnel. Transferred to Blue Star management in 1945, she was purchased by Union Cold Storage the following year and renamed *Royal Star* and given a new funnel. In October 1961 she was sent to Bremer Vulkan at Vegesack to be converted to a motor ship. She was fitted with a larger funnel and renamed *Caledonia Star* under the ownership of Blue Star Line. She arrived at Kaohsiung on 9 December 1971 to be broken up.

Below: Ulster Star Blue Star Line (1959, 10,413grt, 158 x 21m, 17kt)

Built by Harland & Wolff at Belfast in 1959 for the Australian service. She was transferred to Lamport & Holt ownership in 1964 and back to Blue Star the following year. In 1972 she was transferred to the South American route when the four passenger vessels were withdrawn. She arrived at Kaohsiung on 3 October 1979 to be broken up.

Left: Darinian Ellerman & Papayanni (1947, 1,533grt, 83 x 13m, 12kt)

Delivered to Ellerman & Papayanni and also operated for Westcott & Laurence out of London. In 1970 she was sold to Cia. Naviera Evdelia S.A., Panama and renamed *Kostandis Fotinos*, being renamed *Tania Maria* the following year and finally *Nektarios* in 1973. On 16 April 1978 she was wrecked on Perim Island, Aden, and was abandoned.

Below: City of Manchester Ellerman City Lines (1950, 7,583grt, 148 x 19m, 16kt)

She was sold to Kavo Cia Naviera S.A., Panama in 1971, renamed *Kavo Yerakes* and arrived at Kaohsiung on 11 November that year to be broken up.

Opposite above: The temporary container terminal in Gladstone Dock.

Opposite below: A Clan Line vessel prepares to sail from Langton lock.

Above: City of Gloucester Hall Line (1963 ,4,803grt, 132 x 18m, 15kt)
She was built by Wm.Denny & Bros. at Dumbarton. Sold to Lionheart Maritime Inc, Piraeus in 1979, she was renamed *Suerte* and finally broken up at Dalian, China in 1985.

Above: The North Docks system in 1965.

Right: Stirlingshire Houston Line (1945, 6,987grt, 137 x 17m, 12kt)
She was built by Harland & Wolff at Belfast as *Empire Falkland* with Turnbull, Martin as managers. She was acquired by Cayzer Irvine in 1946 and renamed *Stirlingshire* under the management of Houston Line. After twenty years of service with the group she was sold in 1966 and arrived at Bruges for breaking up on 2 September that year.

Opposite below, left: Clan Forbes Clan Line (1961, 9,292grt, 151 x 19m, 16kt)
She was sold in 1968 to the Arya National Shipping Lines S.A., Iran, renamed *Arya Man* and transferred to the Islamic Republic of Iran Shipping Lines in 1980 becoming *Iran Hemmet*. She arrived at Alang on 3 October 1985 to be broken up.

Opposite below, right: Construction of the new Seaforth Terminal in 1960.

Clan Maclennan Clan Line (1948, 6,366grt, 136 x 19m, 15kt)
Launched on 16 September 1947 at the Greenock Dockyard Company. On 2 December 1961 she was in collision with the tanker *British Defender* on the approach to Beira subsequently colliding with the *British Crusader* in fog on the Thames in November 1966. Following this accident she was sent to Smiths at South Shields for repairs. She arrived at Shanghai on 16 September 1971 to be broken up.

The Cunard Line vessels *Media* (1963, 5,586grt) and *Carinthia* (1956, 21,947grt) loading in Huskisson Dock, Liverpool.

Assyria (1950, 8,530grt) with the Mersey Docks & Harbour Board heavy lift crane 'Mammoth' loading a 120-ton stator for shipment to a Canadian power station. On delivery in 1950 *Assyria* completed Cunard Line's 90,000-ton post-war five ship rebuilding programme for the Canadian services. She was sold in 1963 becoming *Laertis*, then *Holy Trinity* in 1970. She was broken up in 1973.

Assyria's sister *Arabia* (1948, 8,632grt) was sold in 1963 and renamed *Onshun*. She arrived at Kaohsiung on 10 May 1972 to be broken up.

Alsatia Cunard Line (1948, 7,226grt, 153 x 20m, 16kt)

She was built by J.L. Thompson & Sons at Sunderland as *Siverplane* for the Silver Line's round-the-world service. Purchased by Cunard Line in 1951, with her sister *Silverbriar*, which was renamed *Andria*. They were initially placed on the Liverpool-New York service and later transferred to the London to Canada route. The two sisters were sold in 1963 to the China Union Lines, Taiwan. *Alsatia* was renamed *Union Freedom* and *Andria* became *Union Faith*.

On 7 April 1969 *Union Faith* collided with three oil barges being towed off New Orleans. The oil ignited and engulfed *Union Faith* and she sank off Poydras Wharf, New Orleans with a loss of twenty-six seaman, including the barge crew. *Union Freedom* was broken up at Kaohsiung in 1977

The Brocklebank cargo vessel *Matra* (1949, 8.954grt) and the Cunard Line vessels *Parthia* (1963, 5,586grt) and *Media* (1963, 5,586grt) loading cargo in Huskisson Dock, Liverpool.

Blue Funnel Line advertisment, 1960.

Radnorshire (1947, 8,295grt) was built as *Achilles* by Caledon at Dundee for the Blue Funnel Line. She Became *Radnorshire* in 1949, *Asphalion* in 1962, *Polyphemus* in 1966, *Asphalion* in 1972 and *Gulf Anchor* in 1975. She arrived at Kaohsiung on 28 April 1979 to be broken up.

Left: Pyrrhus Blue Funnel Line (1949, 10,093grt, 157 x 21m, 19kt)

On 12 November 1964, *Pyrrhus* suffered a serious fire in Huskisson Dock, Liverpool while she was unloading cargo. It took firefighters nearly twenty-four hours to control the blaze and the ship was at risk of capsizing on several occasions. She was repaired and returned to service early the following year. She arrived at Taiwan on 19 September 1972 to be broken up.

Below: Blue Funnel, Glen and Shire Lines sailing schedule, 1961.

THE BLUE FUNNEL, GLEN AND SHIRE LINES

OCEAN STEAM SHIP CO. LTD.   THE CHINA MUTUAL STEAM NAVIGATION CO. LTD.   GLEN LINE LTD.

APPROXIMATE SCHEDULE OF EASTERN PASSENGER SERVICE SAILINGS

1961   *Subject to alteration without notice*

SHIP	Leaves U.K. or Continent	Due Port Said	Due Penang	Due Singapore	Due Manila	Due Hong Kong	Due Japan	SHIP	Leaves U.K. or Continent	Due Port Said	Due Penang	Due Singapore	Due Manila	Due Hong Kong	Due Japan
§ GLENEARN	Jan. 4	Jan. 12	Jan. 26	Feb. 1	—	Feb. 7	Feb. 18	§ GLENGARRY	May 4	May 12	May 26	June 1	—	June 7	June 14
† PELEUS*	Jan. 7	Jan. 21	—	Feb. 3	Feb. 9	Feb. 14	Feb. 20	† PELEUS*	May 6	May 21	—	June 3	June 9	June 14	June 20
† AUTOMEDON	Jan. 10	Jan. 19	Feb. 2	Feb. 4 B	—	Feb. 21	—	† ELPENOR	May 8	May 17	May 31	June 7 I	—	—	—
§ GLENSHIEL	Jan. 11	Jan. 20	—	Feb. 4 B	Feb. 21	Feb. 19	—	† MARON	May 11	May 20	—	June 3 B	—	June 17	—
† ADRASTUS	Jan. 18	Jan. 27	Feb. 10	Feb. 15	—	Feb. 21	Feb. 27	§ RADNORSHIRE	May 11	May 20	—	June 4 B	June 21	June 19	—
† ACHILLES*	Jan. 20	Feb. 2	—	Feb. 16 B	—	—	—	† EUMAEUS	May 18	May 27	June 10	June 15	—	June 21	June 27
§ CARDIGAN-SHIRE	Jan. 20	Jan. 28	Feb. 11	Feb. 17	—	Feb. 23	Mar. 6	† AUTOMEDON*	May 20	June 2	—	June 17 B	—	—	—
† POLYDORUS	Jan. 24	Feb. 2	Feb. 16	Feb. 21	—	Feb. 27	Mar. 5	§ GLENEARN	May 20	May 28	June 11	June 17	—	June 23	July 4
† AUTOLYCUS	Feb. 1	Feb. 10	Feb. 24	Mar. 1	—	Mar. 7	—	† AENEAS	May 20	May 29	June 12	June 19 I	—	June 27	July 3
§ GLENROY	Feb. 4	Feb. 12	Feb. 26	Mar. 4	—	Mar. 10	Mar. 21	† POLYDORUS	May 24	June 2	June 16	June 21	—	—	—
§ CYCLOPS	Feb. 6	Feb. 15	Mar. 1	Mar. 8 I	—	—	—	§ CARDIGAN-SHIRE	June 1	June 10	June 24	June 29	—	July 5	—
† PATROCLUS*	Feb. 7	Feb. 21	—	Mar. 6	Mar. 12	Mar. 17	Mar. 23	† ADRASTUS	June 1	June 10	June 24	June 29	—	July 5	—
† ANTILOCHUS	Feb. 8	Feb. 17	Mar. 5	Mar. 12 I	—	—	—	† PATROCLUS*	June 7	June 21	—	July 4	July 10	July 15	July 21
† MENESTHEUS	Feb. 11	Feb. 20	—	Mar. 6 B	—	Mar. 20	—	† ASCANIUS	June 8	June 17	July 1	July 8 I	—	—	—
† MENELAUS	Feb. 18	Feb. 27	Mar. 12	Mar. 17	—	Mar. 23	Mar. 29	† ACHILLES	June 10	June 19	—	July 5 B	—	July 17	—
† DEMODOCUS*	Feb. 20	Mar. 3	—	Mar. 19 B	—	—	—	§ GLENSHIEL	June 11	June 20	—	July 5 B	July 22	July 20	—
† GLENGYLE	Feb. 20	Mar. 14	Mar. 14	Mar. 20	—	Mar. 26	Apr. 6	† AUTOLYCUS	June 17	June 26	July 10	July 15	—	July 21	July 27
† ATREUS	Feb. 24	Mar. 5	Mar. 19	Mar. 24	—	Mar. 30	Apr. 5	† MENESTHEUS*	June 20	July 3	—	July 17 B	—	—	—
† DOLIUS	Mar. 1	Mar. 10	Mar. 23	Mar. 28	—	Apr. 3	—	† ATREUS	June 24	July 3	July 17	July 22	—	July 28	Aug. 3
§ DENBIGHSHIRE	Mar. 4	Mar. 12	Mar. 26	Apr. 1	—	Apr. 7	Apr. 18	† MENELAUS	July 1	July 10	July 23	July 28	—	Aug. 3	—
† PERSEUS*	Mar. 7	Mar. 21	—	Apr. 3	Apr. 9	Apr. 14	Apr. 20	† ANTILOCHUS	July 3	July 12	July 26	Aug. 2 I	—	—	—
† LAOMEDON	Mar. 8	Mar. 17	Apr. 2	Apr. 9 I	—	—	—	§ GLENGYLE	July 4	July 13	July 26	Aug. 1	—	—	—
† MACHAON	Mar. 11	Mar. 20	—	Apr. 3 B	—	Apr. 17	—	† PERSEUS*	July 7	July 21	—	Aug. 3	Aug. 9	Aug. 14	Aug. 20
† GLENFRUIN	Mar. 11	Mar. 20	—	Apr. 4 B	Apr. 21	Apr. 19	—	§ CYCLOPS	July 8	July 17	July 31	Aug. 7 I	—	—	—
† DIOMED	Mar. 18	Mar. 27	Apr. 9	Apr. 14	—	Apr. 20	Apr. 26	† DEMODOCUS	July 11	July 20	—	Aug. 3 B	—	—	—
† CLYTONEUS	Mar. 18	Mar. 27	Apr. 10	Apr. 17 I	—	—	—	† DOLIUS	July 18	July 27	Aug. 9	Aug. 14	—	Aug. 20	Aug. 26
† ANTENOR*	Mar. 20	Apr. 2	—	Apr. 16 B	—	—	—	§ DENBIGHSHIRE	July 20	July 28	Aug. 11	Aug. 17	—	Aug. 23	Sept. 3
† GLENARTNEY	Mar. 20	Mar. 28	Apr. 11	Apr. 17	—	Apr. 23	May 4	† MACHAON	July 20	Aug. 2	—	Aug. 16 B	—	—	—
† AGAPENOR	Mar. 24	Apr. 2	Apr. 16	Apr. 21	—	Apr. 27	May 3	† AGAPENOR	July 24	Aug. 2	Aug. 16	Aug. 21	—	Aug. 27	Sept. 2
† LYCAON	Apr. 1	Apr. 10	Apr. 24	Apr. 29	—	May 5	—	† DIOMED	Aug. 1	Aug. 10	Aug. 23	Aug. 28	—	Sept. 3	—
§ GLENORCHY	Apr. 4	Apr. 12	Apr. 26	May 2	—	May 6	May 17	† GLENARTNEY	Aug. 4	Aug. 12	Aug. 26	Sept. 1	—	Sept. 7	Sept. 18
† PYRRHUS*	Apr. 7	Apr. 21	—	May 4	May 10	May 15	May 21	† PYRRHUS*	Aug. 7	Aug. 21	—	Sept. 3	Sept. 9	Sept. 14	Sept. 20
† MEMNON	Apr. 11	Apr. 20	—	May 4 B	—	May 18	—	† ANTENOR	Aug. 11	Aug. 20	—	Sept. 3 B	—	—	—
§ GLENFINLAS	Apr. 11	Apr. 20	—	May 5 B	May 22	May 20	—	† GLENFRUIN	Aug. 11	Aug. 20	—	Sept. 4 B	Sept. 8	Sept. 14	Sept. 20
† LAERTES	Apr. 18	Apr. 27	May 11	May 16	—	May 22	May 28	† LYCAON	Aug. 18	Aug. 27	Sept. 10	Sept. 15	—	Sept. 21	Sept. 27
§ MELAMPUS*	Apr. 20	Mar. 3	—	May 17 B	—	—	—	§ GLENORCHY	Aug. 20	Aug. 28	Sept. 11	Sept. 17	—	Sept. 21	Oct. 3
§ BRECONSHIRE	Apr. 20	Apr. 28	May 12	May 18	—	May 24	June 4	† MEMNON*	Aug. 19	Sept. 1	—	Sept. 15 B	—	—	—
§ ANCHISES	Apr. 24	May 3	May 17	May 22	—	May 28	June 3	† ANCHISES	Aug. 24	Sept. 2	Sept. 16	Sept. 21	—	Sept. 27	Oct. 3
† AJAX	May 1	May 10	May 23	May 28	—	June 3	—								

† Blue Funnel ships sailing from Birkenhead.   ‡ Blue Funnel ships sailing from Amsterdam.   * Via Rotterdam.

§ Glen Line ships sailing from London.   I Takes passengers to Indonesia.   B Via Bangkok.

No. 117 JANUARY, 1961   PRINTED IN ENGLAND   1.85M

Right: Blue Funnel Line Cruise advertisement.

Below: Mentor Blue Funnel Line (1945, 7,642grt, 135 x 19m, 15kt)
She was built as *Carthage Victory* and was renamed *Mentor* when she was purchased by the Ocean Steamship Company in 1947. In 1967 she was sold to Seawave Navigation Corporation, Greece and renamed *Vita, Viva* in 1969, *Syra* in 1971 and broken up at Split in September that year.

S.A.Victory South African Marine Corporation (1945, 7,605grt, 139 x 19m, 15kt)
Launched as *Westbrook Victory*, she became *Verelegen* in 1947, *South African Victory* in 1961,
S.A.Victory in 1966 and was broken up at Kaohsiung in 1969.

South African Seafarer South African Marine Corporation (1950, 8,101grt, 156 x 20m, 15kt)
Built as *Clan Shaw*, she sailed on her maiden voyage from Birkenhead to Durban, Lourenco Marques
and Beira on 25 January 1950. She represented the Clan Line at the Coronation Review on 15 June
1953 when the No.4 tween-deck hold was converted to a luxury lounge. Transferred to the Springbok
Line in January 1960 and renamed *Steenbok*. She was moved to Safmarine the following year and
became *South African Seafarer*. On 30 June 1966 she anchored off the Cape in storm force conditions.
When the winds abated she was told to enter the port and grounded near Green Point Light and broke
her back. The sixty-three crew and twelve passengers were taken off by helicopter and she was declared
a total loss, later being dismantled where she lay.

The Birkenhead dock system.

The coal unloading berth at Gladstone Dock.

Opposite: New Zealand Shipping Company's *Hinakura* (1949, 11,272grt) loads cargo at Gladstone Dock in 1964. She was given a Federal Lines' funnel in 1966, painted in P&O colours in 1973 and broken up at Kaohsiung the following year.

Above: Cheshire Bibby Line (1927, 10,550grt, 147 x 18m, 16kt)
She was built by the Fairfield Shipbuilding & Engineering Co. at Glasgow and was launched on 20 April 1927 as the sister of *Shropshire*, which was built the previous year. On 3 September 1939 when war broke out, she was ordered to Calcutta where she was converted to an Armed Merchant Cruiser, HMS *Cheshire*, and was sent on North Atlantic patrols. On 14 October 1940 she was torpedoed by U-137, west of Ireland and an attempt was made to tow her to safety but she went aground at Carrickfergus. Repairs were made by the Liverpool Salvage Association and she was brought into Belfast and then to Gladstone Dock at Liverpool.

On 14 March 1942 she stopped the German raider *Doggerbank* and on July 24 that summer she towed Lambert Bros. *Temple Inn*, which had lost its propeller in Point Noire, West Africa. She was torpedoed again in the North Atlantic and survived the attack. Following repairs it was decided that she would be converted to a troopship and on 7 June 1944 together with *Lancashire, Devonshire* and *Worcestershire* she arrived at Juno Beach, with troops from the Thames. *Cheshire* continued to be used as a troopship during 1945 and on 25 September 1946 she brought residents back to Gibraltar who had been evacuated to Northern Ireland in 1940.

Cheshire was returned to the Bibby Line on 5 October 1948 and was refitted at Liverpool. Her first sailing was from Liverpool to Sydney on 9 August the following year. She was used as a troopship during the Korean War in 1953 and was laid up in Liverpool following the completion of her final trooping duties in 1957. She was sold to J.Cashmore at Newport, Monmouthshire later that year, to be broken up.

Left: Bibby Line short sea voyages advert.

Below: Warwickshire Bibby Line (1948, 8,903grt, 146 x 18m, 16kt)
Built by the Fairfield Shipbuilding & Engineering Company at Govan and sailed on her maiden voyage from Birkenhead to Burma on 5 September 1948. When the Bibby Line passenger service ceased in 1965, she was sold to the Aegean Steam Navigation Company, Typaldos Bros, Greece and converted into a car ferry for the Piraeus to Crete route and renamed Hania. In 1966, following the collapse of Typaldos Bros., she was laid up and scrapped.

Above: Eastern Prince Prince Line (1950, 8,827grt, 144 x 19m, 14kt)
Built on the River Tyne by Vickers Armstrong, she was delivered to Prince Line in September 1950. She was chartered to Shaw Savill Line in 1960 and renamed *Bardic*. She was purchased by Bibby Line in 1964 together with her sister ship *Cingalese Prince. Eastern Prince* was renamed *Staffordshire* and her sister became *Gloucestershire*. On 30 November 1970, while on voyage from Liverpool to Rangoon, she experienced engine problems and was diverted to Colombo where she was sold and arrived in tow at Hong Kong to be broken up on 6 March the following year.

Below: Bank Line and Harrison Line vessels in Liverpool Docks.

Runswick Headlam & Son (1956, 6,229grt, 145 x 19m, 14kt)
She was renamed *Margaret H* in 1972, *Osia Irini Chrysovalandou III* in 1977 and was broken up in 1978.

Vessels laid up in Brocklebank Dock, Liverpool during the seamans' strike in 1966: *Willi Rickmers* (1954, 7,003grt), *Aureol* (1951, 14,083grt), *Apapa* (1948, 11,607grt) and *City of Liverpool* (1949, 7,612grt) berthed in Brocklebank Dock.

Iberic Shaw, Savill Line (1961, 11,248grt, 156 x 22m, 17kt)
She was built by Alex Stephen & Sons at Glasgow and was transferred to Royal Mail Lines in 1976 and renamed *Deseado*. Sold to Greek interests in 1981 becoming *San George* and was broken up two years later

A Ghanaian Black Star Line vessel unloading cargo at Liverpool.

Left: Booker Venture Booker Line (1961, 8,227grt, 143 x 19m, 14kt)
She became *Caribbean Memories* in 1978, *Thanic* in 1980, *Trader* in 1986 and was finally broken up at Alang in 1986.

Below: Benreoch Ben Line (1952, 10,142grt, 154 x 20m, 17kt)
She was renamed *Tudis* in 1976 and broken up three years later.

Opposite above: Repairs are carried out to an F.C.Strick Line vessel in the Liverpool dock system in 1963.

Below: Sarmiento Pacific Steam Navigation (1945, 6,393grt, 142 x 19m, 15kt)

Sister to *Samanco* which was also built by Harland & Wolff at Belfast. *Sarmiento* was completed two years after her sister and traded on the Company's services to South America until she was sold to Monomachos Cia Nav. S.A., Piraeus in 1969 and became *Monomachos*. Sold again to the Eagle Ocean Shipping Company of Famagusta, Cyprus in 1970 she was renamed *Gladiator* and was broken up at Shanghai in 1971 following a voyage from Havana where she left on 28 February.

Ebro Royal Mail Lines (1952, 7,784grt, 135 x 17m, 14kt)
Ebro was another product of Harland & Wolff at Belfast and was completed by them in June 1952. She was sold by Royal Mail Lines to Fortune Maritime of Hong Kong in 1969 and renamed *Fortune Victory*. Finally sold to the Union of Burma Five Star Line at Rangoon the following year, she became *Kalemyo* and was broken up at Tsingtao in 1978.

Beaverelm Canadian Pacific Line (1960, 3,964grt, 101 x 15m, 14kt)
She was built by Moss Vaerft & Dokk A/S , Norway and launched as *Roga* for Akties, Asplund Moss to sail their Riga to Conakry route. Purchased by Canadian Pacific in 1962, she was given the name *Beaverelm* and sailed on her first voyage for them leaving Antwerp for Bremen, Hamburg, Montreal and Toronto on 1 September that year.

She was sold by Canadian Pacific in September 1971 to the Nan Yang Shipping Company, Mogadishu, and flew the Somali flag as *Hengshan*. In 1976 she was owned by the Fortune Sea Transport Corporation of Panama who sold her to the China Ocean Shipping Company, People's Republic of China the following year and she was renamed *Yong Kang*. She was broken up in 1992.

Beaverfir Canadian Pacific Line (1961, 4,539grt, 105 x 15m, 15kt)

She was built by Sarpsberg Mek. Vekstad A/S, Greaker, Oslo and acquired by Canadian Pacific while she was being built. Launched on 22 March 1961 to operate with five other vessels on the Great Lakes service via the St. Lawrence Seaway. She left Antwerp for Quebec and Montreal on her maiden voyage on 7 July. Her sailings were extended to Toronto and she became the first Canadian Pacific deep-sea vessel to visit the Lakes.

She was sold to Arion Shipping of Monrovia in April 1972 renamed *Arion*, before being sold in 1975 to become *Manaure II* for Linera Manaure Cia. Anon of Venezuela. Sold again in 1981 to Grand Cayman interests becoming *Anden* and while owned by Intercontinental Maritima S.A. she dragged her anchor during a storm off Acajutla on 20 September 1982 and was blown ashore on Barra de Santiago when sixteen of her crew of twenty-six were lost.

The Elders & Fyffes vessels *Golfito* (1949, 8,740grt) and *Camito* (1956, 8,687grt) operated from Garston, Southampton and Greenock to Jamaica direct or via Barbados and Trinidad, and also to the British Cameroons. *Golfito* was broken up at Faslane in 1971.

Above: Albert Dock in 1960. *Below: Benarty* Ben Line (1963, 10,294grt, 155 x 20m, 18kt)
She was renamed *Kota Petani* in 1981 and broken up at Kaohsiung in 1985.

ICI vessels in the north dock system at Liverpool.

Manchester Regiment Manchester Liners (1947, 7,638grt, 141 x 18m, 14kt)

She was launched by the wife of the colonel of the Manchester Regiment on 16 October 1946 and was delivered to Manchester Liners in February the following year. Sold to Astro Tropica Cia. Nav. S.A. in 1969 and renamed *Azure Coast II*, she was purchased by Li-Ho Shipping (Singapore) Ltd. in 1971 and became *Pu Gor*. She arrived at Kaohsiung on 24 November that year to be broken up.

Manchester Spinner Manchester Liners (1952, 7,815grt, 142 x 18m, 15kt)
She was built and delivered by Cammell Laird at Birkenhead in July 1952. On 30 March 1954 she docked at Montreal without the aid of tugs, which were still icebound. It was the earliest ever opening of the St Lawrence Seaway. She was sold to Estia Cia. Nav. S.A., Piraeus in 1968 and became *Estia* and finally sank after an engine room explosion off the coast of Somalia on 25 November 1971.

Geestcape Geest Industries (1966, 7,679grt, 149 x 19m, 21kt)
She became the *Nyombe* in 1975 and was broken up in 1982.

Hopepeak (1963, 7,457grt) discharging grain at the Homepride Flour Mills in the East Float at Birkenhead in 1968. She was owned by the Hopemount Steam Ship Company until 1969 when she was renamed *Natalie*, becoming *Pegasus* in 1981 and was broken up at Xingang in China where she arrived on 10 May 1985.

Cheviot Bamburgh Shipping Co. (1961, 13,082grt, 160 x 21m, 12kt)
She was sold in 1977 and renamed *Dapo Trader*, *Trader* in 1984 and was broken up in Setubal later that year.

British Gunner B.P. Tanker Co. Ltd (1954, 10,076grt, 158 x 20m, 13kt)
Renamed *Clyde Gunner* in 1961, *British Gunner* in 1963 she was broken up in Vinaroz in 1972.

Opposite, above and below: Karnak Moss Hutchison Line (1948, 3,198grt, 112 x 16m, 13kt)
She was sold in 1971 and renamed *Eudocia* finally being broken up in Bombay in 1981.

Above: Moss Hutchison vessels loading cargo at Alexandra Dock, Liverpool in 1962.

Opposite below: Essex Federal Steam Nav. Co. (1954, 10,936grt, 160 x 21m, 16kt)
Built by John Brown & Co. on the Clyde, she was the sister ship of *Otaki*. Both vessels were sold in 1975 and *Essex* became *Golden Gulf* owned by Guan Guan Shipping Ltd of Singapore and was broken up at Gadani Beach in 1977. Her sister, *Otaki*, was sold to Roussos Brothers of Piraeus and while she was being refitted as *Mahmout* at Perama she suffered a serious fire and was declared a total loss and was broken up at Izmir in Turkey in 1984.

Above: Somerset (1962, 10,027grt), *Middlesex* (1953, 8,284grt) and *Huntingdon* (1948, 11,282grt)
in Gladstone Dock, Liverpool
Somerset was sold to Damariki Shipping Corporation, Greece in 1980 and renamed *Aegean Sky* before being broken up at Chittagong in 1984. *Middlesex* was transferred to British India Line in 1965 and renamed *Jelunga*, then *Strathleven* in 1975 and was broken up at Gadani Beach in 1978. *Huntingdon* was transferred to P&O's General Cargo Division in 1973 and was broken up at Hualien, Taiwan, in 1975.

Blue Star and Ellerman Line vessels load cargo in Langton Dock.

Axina Shell Tankers (1958, 12,293grt, 170 x 21m, 15kt)
She was broken up at Kaohsiung in 1978.

three

Mersey Ferries
Coastal Vessels
Tugs and
Dredgers

Lily Wallasey Corporation (1901, 514grt, 47 x 13m)
She was built by John Jones at Liverpool and launched on 11 September 1900. *Lily* was completed in January 1901, was sold and renamed *Failte* in 1927. She was wrecked near Bunessan on 8 May 1943.

Wallasey Wallasey Corporation (1927, 606grt, 46 x 15m, 12kt).
Built by Caledon Shipbuilding & Engineering Co.Ltd. at Dundee and launched on 31 May 1927. She was converted to oil-burning in 1946 and was sold to Van Heyghen before being broken up at Ghent in 1964.

Birkenhead Corporation ferry *Bidston* (1933, 487grt) berthing at Liverpool Landing Stage. She was broken up at Cork in 1962.

The high speed catamaran *Highland Seabird* (1976, 202grt) was chartered in 1982 to evaluate the use of this type of vessel on ferry services on the Mersey. On 20 December 1982, heavy winds and a fast tide swept her behind the Pier Head Landing Stage and she was there for about forty-five minutes, until being rescued by the *Royal Iris*, which pulled her clear. The trials proved unsuccessful and she was returned to her owners Western Ferries Limited. She became *Trident II* in 1985, *Cap Suroit* in 1990 and *Dumont D'Urville* in 1997.

Opposite, above and below: Royal Daffodil II was built by Cammell Laird at Birkenhead in 1934 and cost £44,790.

She was one of the most popular Mersey ferries as she operated dance cruises. During the Second World War she was used to stand by troopships in case there was the need for a fast evacuation and she also functioned as a ferry. On the night of 8 May 1941 she was hit by a bomb at Seacombe and sank. It took a year to salvage her and she was finally able to return to ferry duties on 2 June 1943. After the war she was engaged on ferry services and pleasure trips. In January 1956 an attempt was made to sink her by opening a valve in her main engine room but she was saved by the watchman on duty. In 1957 she was renamed *St Hilary*, to enable a new vessel to take her name, and she was used as a summer relief vessel before sale in 1962. She was towed to the shipbreakers by the tug *Ocean Bull*, with the Birkenhead Corporation ferry *Claughton* (below) on 21 September 1962.

Above: Francis Storey (1922, 464grt) was built by the Ailsa Shipbuilding & Engineering Co. and was named after a chairman of the Wallasey Ferries Committee who died before the ship was delivered. She carried a four-inch wide purple mourning-band on the outside of her bulwark for her first year in service. She was painted with a grey hull and buff funnel and carried out ferry services and river cruises. *Francis Storey* and her sister *J. Farley* were taken over by the Admiralty in 1943. The *J. Farley* was on operations around Milford Haven and *Francis Storey* was based in Liverpool Bay. In February 1951 she was sold to the Cork Harbour Commissioners, renamed *Killarney* and was broken up in 1960 by Shirling & Sons at Cork.

Royal Iris II (1932, 591grt) was built by Harland & Wolff at Govan and her engines were supplied by D&W Henderson at Glasgow. She had a reputation of being a slower ship than her sisters and helped to maintain the ferry service during the Second World War. The suffix II was dropped from her name in 1947 and was renamed *St Hilary* in 1950 in preparation for the delivery of the new *Royal Iris* from Denny's of Dumbarton. She was sold to Stolk NV. in 1956 and sailed from the Mersey to Holland where she was fitted with new diesel engines and converted to carry forty vehicles between Hellvoetsluis and Middleharnis. She was renamed *Haringvliet* in 1957 under the management of the Rotterdamsche Tramweg Maatschappy, a company engaged in ferry and railway services in the south west of Holland. After initial problems over manoeuvrabilty were resolved she remained on the service until 1971 when she became *Schellingerland,* in service between Terschelling and Harlingen. In 1981 she was sold to the Gidenay Navigation Company of Kyrenia, Cyprus and she was renamed *Girne.* A stern ramp was installed in addition to the side loading facilities. However, the firm experienced financial difficulties and *Girne* was arrested on 4 November 1982 at Famagusta. The vessel remained at the port until 5 June the following year, when she left Famagusta still under arrest, and was later seen at the French port of La Seyne, near Toulon, where she was still laid up in 1992.

Opposite above: Birkenhead and Wallasey Ferries at Liverpool Landing Stage.

Opposite below: Rock Ferry Ferry Terminal.

Above and below: The Mersey Ferry *Woodchurch* (1960, 464grt) in the livery applied for the Festival Gardens service in 1985.

JUNE 1 – SEPTEMBER 8 '85

FESTIVAL GARDENS

FERRY TIMETABLE

The Mersey Ferries

Sponsored by Merseyside County Council

CRUISE ALONG TO THE

FESTIVAL GARDENS

Ferry trips will depart most weekends, and on school and bank holidays (until September 8th) from the Pier Head and travel via Woodside to Otterspool, close to the Festival Gardens site, returning to the Pier Head.
Times will vary according to tides.

There will be a single fare of 40p adults and 25p child

With Special COMMEMORATIVE FERRY TICKETS

Zone Tickets, Saveaway Tickets and Concessionary Passes are not valid on the Festival Gardens' service. The dates and times of the Festival Gardens' service may be altered without prior notice.

Wallasey Corporation ferry *Egremont* (1952, 566grt) on a windy and rough day on the Mersey in 1960.

Leasowe (1951, 567grt) berths at New Brighton in May 1954.

Royal Daffodil II (1958, 609grt) berthing at Liverpool Landing Stage in 1962. She was renamed *Royal Daffodil* in 1968 and sold to Greek interests in 1977 becoming *Ioulis Keas II, Agia Kyriaki* in 1992, and *Dolphin I* in 1994. On 7 November 2007 about twenty miles from Cape Andreas, Cyprus, she sustained steering failure during heavy weather and sank. She was on passage between Mersin and Famagusta.

Opposite above: Ioulis Keas II. (John Williamson).

Opposite below: Royal Iris was built by Wm Denny & Bros at Dumbarton in 1951. She was a twin-screw, diesel-electric vessel which ran her trials on the Clyde on 28 April 1951 being delivered to Wallasey Corporation a week later. She was designed as a dual-purpose vessel spending time on the ferry services from Seacombe and New Brighton to Liverpool and for cruises on the river. She operated her last cruise on 12 January 1991 and also carried out a special Zeebrugge Commemorative cruise on 21 April that year. *Royal Iris* was sold for use as a restaurant ship in 1994, she moved to Cardiff in 1995 and to London in 1998.

The dance floor on the *Royal Iris*.

It's a **WONDERFUL**
day out on a . . .

DAY CRUISE to LLANDUDNO and MENAI BRIDGE aboard ST. TUDNO and ST. SEIRIOL

The LIVERPOOL & NORTH WALES STEAMSHIP CO. LTD
40 CHAPEL STREET · LIVERPOOL · 3 · CENtral 1653

Right and below: The Liverpool & North Wales vessels *St Tudno* (1926, 2,326grt), *St Seriol* (1931, 1,586grt) and *St Trillo* (1936, 314grt) operated day cruises from Liverpool to Llandudno and Menai Bridge and cruises from Llandudno. The company operated until 1961 when it went into voluntary liquidation and the two larger vessels were sold for scrap. *St Trillo* was converted into a floating restaurant in 1972 and was broken up in Dublin in 1975.

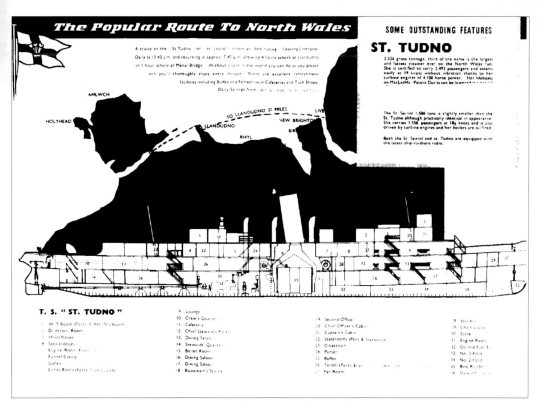

The Popular Route To North Wales

A cruise on the 'St Tudno' or 'St Seiriol' makes an ideal outing. Leaving Liverpool Daily at 10.45 a.m. and returning at approx. 7.40 p.m. allowing 4 hours ashore at Llandudno or 1 hour ashore at Menai Bridge. Without a care in the world you can do as you please and you'll thoroughly enjoy every minute. There are excellent refreshment facilities including Buffet and Refreshment Cafeterias and Tuck Shops.
Daily Sailings from

SOME OUTSTANDING FEATURES

ST. TUDNO

2,326 gross tonnage, third of the name is the largest and fastest steamer ever on the North Wales run. She is certified to carry 2,493 passengers and steams easily at 19 knots without vibration thanks to her turbine engines of 4,100 horse power. Her lifeboats on MacLachla Patent Davits can be lowered at a second.

The St. Seiriol 1,586 tons is slightly smaller than the St. Tudno although practically identical in appearance. She carries 1,556 passengers at 18½ knots and is also driven by turbine engines and her boilers are oil fired.

Both the St. Seiriol and St. Tudno are equipped with the latest ship-to-shore radio.

T. S. " ST. TUDNO "

1. W. T. Room (Ports Buffet/Starboard)
2. Directors Room
3. Wheelhouse
4. Stewardesses
   Engine Room Fittings
   Funnel Casing
   Galley
   Ladies Room (Forward Tuck Shop)
9. Lounge
10. Crew's Quarters
11. Cafeteria
12. Chief Steward's Pantry
13. Dining Saloon
14. Stewards Quarters
15. Boiler Room
16. Dining Saloon
17. Dining Saloon
18. Boatswain's Stores
19. Second Officer
20. Chief Officer's Cabin
21. Captain's Cabin
22. Staterooms (Port & Starboard)
23. Cloakroom
24. Purser
25. Buffet
26. Toilets (Port), Engine Room
27. Fan Room
28. Scullers
29. Chain Locker
30. Store
31. Engine Room
32. Oil and Fuel Tank
33. No. 3 Hold
34. No. 2 Hold
35. Bow Rudder
36. Store

119

France, Spain and Gibraltar

September 16 — September 29

The "AVALON" cruise goes south to Spain, September 16-September 29, sailing from Harwich and Dover on September 16 with shore excursions at Bordeaux, Seville, Gibraltar and Santander – arriving back at Harwich on September 29.

Sail south to the sun in September. The first port of call is Bordeaux in France before cruising down the warm Atlantic waters to the inland port of Seville in Southern Spain. The "Avalon" will be the largest cruise ship to visit Seville. Nearby is Gibraltar, the next stop, where the Mediterranean begins and where you can see the mountains of Morocco across the narrow strait which separates Europe from Africa. On the way home there's one more place to visit – Santander – a beautiful and elegant beach resort city on Spain's scenic north coast.

BORDEAUX: This spacious city is beautifully situated on a majestic bend of the Garonne river in the heart of one of the greatest wine-producing areas in the world. Bordeaux is not only famous for its many excellent types of wines, it is also justly famed for superb food and good living. This makes it a very popular place for travellers and tourists.

SEVILLE: In the heart of the Sherry country, in Southern Spain, this city reflects everything that is typical of Spanish life and history. Its architecture is a beautiful combination of buildings that were left by the Moors and the splendours of the 16th and 17th centuries when Spain was colonising the New World. The people of Seville take advantage of their warm climate to stroll a great amount, particularly at night, thereby adding much gaiety and colour for visitors to enjoy.

GIBRALTAR: This British naval and military base is on a rocky peninsula which is connected to the mainland of Spain. The town itself is a gay one with tourist facilities galore. There is a new casino, cable cars for scenic rides.

There's a lot to see and do in Gibraltar and one of its unique attractions are the famous Barbary apes which roam free on the Rock slopes.

SANTANDER: This fashionable resort stands in a mountainous region on a peninsula between the sea and a picturesque little bay. A lovely setting! The city has an elegant charm with its well-cared-for parks, fine restaurants, its casino and superb sandy beach. There are many other attractions in Santander – the cathedral, museums and art galleries and fine buildings – but mainly it's a pleasant place to relax in the sun.

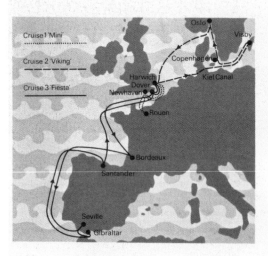

Cruise 1 'Mini'
Cruise 2 'Viking'
Cruise 3 'Fiesta'

September FIESTA cruise Itinerary	13/14 days		
Saturday	Sept 16th	Harwich	dep 14.45
		Dover	arr 18.45
		Dover	dep 20.45
Sunday	Sept 17th	Cruising	
Monday	Sept 18th	Bordeaux	arr 17.00
Tuesday	Sept 19th	Bordeaux	dep 13.00
Wednesday	Sept 20th	Cruising	
Thursday	Sept 21st	Cruising	
Friday	Sept 22nd	Seville	arr 08.00
Saturday	Sept 23rd	Seville	dep 15.00
Sunday	Sept 24th	Gibraltar	arr 07.00
		Gibraltar	dep 18.00
Monday	Sept 25th	Cruising	
Tuesday	Sept 26th	Santander	arr 18.00
Wednesday	Sept 27th	Santander	dep 18.00
Thursday	Sept 28th	Cruising	
Friday	Sept 29th	Dover	arr 13.00
		Dover	dep 14.30
		Harwich	arr 18.30

Opposite and above: British Rail's *Avalon* (1963, 6,584grt) in the East Float at Birkenhead. She was built by Alex. Stephen & Sons at Linthouse and her launch date was delayed until 7 May because of a strike. She cost £2 million and she replaced *Duke of York* on the Harwich to Hook of Holland route. *Avalon* was also designed for off-season cruising with berths for 320 one-class passengers and was registered to sail as far as Gibraltar. This was later extended and in 1966 she cruised to Tangier. In 1966 she was chartered by Ellerman-Wilson due to the late delivery on their new vessel *Spero* from Cammell Laird & Co. at Birkenhead. In 1974 she was made redundant by the arrival of *St Edmund* and was converted to a car ferry by Swan, Hunter Ship Repairers at North Shields on the River Tyne. Two car decks and stern doors were fitted allowing a capacity of 200 cars. In 1975 she replaced *Caledonian Princess* on the Fishguard-Rosslaire route and was relieved on the Holyhead to Dun Laoghaire route in 1976 when she collided with the pier at Holyhead on 17 March and had to be sent to Birkenhead for repairs. On 1 January 1979 she was transferred to the ownership of Sealink U.K. Limited and was replaced by *Stena Normandica*. *Avalon* was moved to Holyhead being used as their relief vessel until 1980 when she was laid up at Barrow and sold to the Seafaith Navigation Company, Cyprus, under the name *Valon*. On 22 January the following year she arrived at Gadani Beach to be broken up.

Above: King Orry (1946, 2,485grt) and *Lady of Mann* (1930, 3,104grt) in drydock at Liverpool.

Left: Ben-my-Chree (1927, 2,586grt) in drydock at Liverpool, 1960.

، anu 1or ɔ monɪns petween Uctober 1st and April 30th	£15
Valid for 6 months between October 1st and April 30th	£24

CONTRACTS AVAILABLE ON ALL THE COMPANY'S ADVERTISED SERVICES INCLUDING ANY OF ITS ADVERTISED EXCURSIONS

SEASON — May 21st to September 13th inclusive	£37
SIX MONTHS	£42
TWELVE MONTHS	£62

CONTRACTS AVAILABLE ON THE COMPANY'S ADVERTISED SERVICES BETWEEN :-

LIVERPOOL AND LLANDUDNO	SEASON	£20
LIVERPOOL AND LLANDUDNO also Cruises ex Llandudno		£25
LLANDUDNO AND DOUGLAS	SEASON	£16
LLANDUDNO AND DOUGLAS also Cruises ex Llandudno		£23
ARDROSSAN AND DOUGLAS	SEASON	£20
BELFAST AND DOUGLAS ... ...、 ...	.,	£20
DUBLIN AND DOUGLAS	,,	£20
HEYSHAM AND DOUGLAS	,,	£10
CRUISES FROM LLANDUDNO		£10

SPECIAL DAY EXCURSION VOUCHERS

10 Contract Vouchers (extendible on request) available for Day Excursions between :

LIVERPOOL AND DOUGLAS	£16
LLANDUDNO AND DOUGLAS	£13

Above: The Isle of Man Steam Packet Contract Application Form, 1971.
Below: Isle of Man Steam Packet Sailing List.

Above: Mountwood (1960, 464grt), *Snaefell* (1948, 2,489grt), *Mona's Isle* (1951, 2,491grt), *Tynwald* (1947, 2,493grt) and *Manxman* (1955, 2,495grt) laid up in Morpeth Dock at Birkenhead in 1962.

Opposite below: Manx Maid (1962, 2,724grt) in the course of demolition at Garston Docks on the River Mersey in 1986.

Right: Snaefell (1948, 2,489grt) off Alfred lock at Birkenhead at the end of the 1963 summer season.

Below: Lady of Mann (1930, 3,104grt)

Above: Lady of Mann (1930, 3,104grt) passes *Manx Maid* (1962, 2,724grt) off Princess Landing Stage. The Wallasey Ferry *Leasowe* is seen heading for New Brighton Pier from Liverpool.

Left: A view of *Be-my-Chree* (1966, 2,762grt) being prepared for an early morning sailing to Douglas in 1966.

Opposite above: Lady Leinster B&I Line (1912, 2,284grt, 325 x 42m)
Built by Harland & Wolff at Belfast, she was launched on 7 September 1911 as *Patriot* for the Belfast Steamship Company Ltd. She was transferred to the British & Irish Steam Packet Co. in 1930 and renamed *Lady Leinster*, becoming *Lady Connaught* in 1938. In 1940 she was damaged by mines and was abandoned to the underwriters the following year. She was purchased from the underwriters and converted to a livestock carrier in 1942 before becoming a hospital ship in 1944.

She was sent to Harland & Wolff in 1946 to be converted to a cruise ship and after her transfer to Coast Lines, the following year she was renamed *Lady Killarney*. She survived until 1956 when she was broken up at Port Glasgow.

Below: Coast Lines *Irish Coast* (1952, 3,824grt) and *Leinster* (1948, 4,115grt) in Princess Dock, Liverpool. *Irish Coast* was operated by Coast Lines until 1968 when she was sold and renamed *Orpheus, Semiramis II, Achilleus* and *Apollon II* in 1969. She became *Regency* in 1981 and was broken up in 1989.

Belfast Steamship Company's *Ulster Monarch* (1929, 3,815grt)

Above, left and right: Ulster Prince (1937, 4,303grt) loading at Princess Landing Stage on a rare summer daylight sailing to Belfast.

Ulster Prince (1937, 4,303grt) moving through the Birkenhead Dock system in 1966 to be laid up in Morpeth Dock. She was launched as *Leinster* for the service from Liverpool to Dublin and was transferred to the Belfast route in 1946 when she was also renamed *Ulster Prince*. In 1966 she was replaced on that service by a new car ferry of the same name and became *Ulster Prince I*. Sold to the Epirotiki Steam Ship Company in 1968 she became *Adria* and was renamed *Odysseus* in 1969. She arrived at Glasgow on 22 July 1977 to be laid up and was sold to Shipbreaking Industries at Faslane, where she arrived on 2 October 1979.

Above: British & Irish Lines *Meath* (1960, 1,558grt), *Munster* (1948, 4,142grt) and *Leinster* (1948, 4,115grt) loading in Princess Dock, Liverpool.

REPRESENTATIVE
VESSELS
from the fleets of
COAST
LINES
and
Associated Companies

Opposite below: Representative vessels of the fleets of Coat Lines and associated companies. 1.*Lairds Oak*. 2. *Freshfield*. 3. *Saxon Queen*. 4. *British Coast*. 5. *Matabele Coast*. 6. *Inniscarra*. 7. *Rowanfield*. 8. *Channel Coast*. 9. *Adriatic Coast*. 10. *Iberian Coast*. 11. *Dundalk*. 12. *Cheshire Coast*. 13. *Ulster Weaver*. 14. *Northumbrian Coast*. 15. *Fife Coast*. 16. *Hadrian Coast*. 17. *Brookmount*. 18. *Lairdsglen*. 19. *Jersey Coast*. 20. *Balmoral Queen*. 21. *Brentfield*. 22. *Innisfallen*. 23. *Ulster Prince*. 24. *Irish Coast*. 25. *Munster*. 26. *Royal Scotsman*. 27. *Ulster Premier*. 28. *Laird's Loch*. 29. *Caledonian Coast*. 30. *Netherlands Coast*. 31. *Kilkenny*

Above: Artist's impression of the new Burns & Laird car ferry *Lion*, which was built at Birkenhead for the Ardrossan-Belfast service. P&O took over the line in 1971 and she made her last sailing on the route on 12 February 1976. *Lion* was transferred to P&O Normandy Ferries' Dover-Boulogne service in April that year and the European Ferries Group took over Normandy Ferries in 1985. *Lion* was used briefly on the Portsmouth-le Havre service, prior to being sold to Greek Cypriot owners and renamed *Baroness M*. In 1987 she was renamed *Portelet*, and reverted to *Baroness M* in 1989. On 24 February 1990 she was attacked by a gunboat thirty miles off Jounich on a voyage from Larnica and one passenger died. She sailed from Greece to Indonesia on 24 January 1997 and was operating as the *Adinda Lestari 101* until 2004 when she was sold and broken up.

Above: Ulster Queen Belfast Steamship Company (1967, 4,270grt, 115 x 16m, 17.5kt)
She was sold in 1982 and renamed *Med Sea, Al-Eddin* and *Al-Kahera* in 1987, *Poseidonia* in
1988 and *La Patria* in 2000. She became *Poseidonia* again in 2002 and *Al Kahfain* in 2005. On a voyage from
Hurghada to Jeddah on 1 November 2005 she suffered a serious fire and after being taken in tow she sank.

Opposite below: Ulster Prince Belfast Steamship Company (1967, 4,270grt, 115 x 16m, 17.5kt)
Sold in 1982 becoming *Lady M, Tangpakorn* in 1985, *Long Hu* in 1987. *Macmosa* in 1988, *Neptunia* in 1994, *Panther* in 1995 and *Vatan* in 2000. She was sold to Manar Marine Services in 2000, renamed *Manar* and was broken up at Alang in 2004.

Above: Leinster was launched on 19 November 1968 at the Verolme Dockyard in Cork for the British & Irish Steam Packet Co.'s service from Liverpool to Dublin. She was renamed *Innisfallen* in 1980 and was sold to Strintzis Lines in 1986, when she also became *Ionian Sun*. In 1990 she was used on the Swansea-Cork route and was chartered to Cotunav (Tunisia) and renamed *Chams* in 1993. She was also became *Ionian Sun* in 1993 and was sold to Marco Shipping Agency in 2001 being renamed *Merdif*. She was broken up in 2004.

Munster was built by Nobiskrug GmbH, Rendsburg, in 1968 and sailed on her maiden voyage from Liverpool to Dublin on 15 May. She remained on the service until 1983 when she was sold to Petra Navigation Agencies and renamed *Farah* and then *Farah I*. In 1990, following various sales to companies in Jordan and Malta she was sold to Dalian Steam Shipping Co., renamed *Tian Peng* and was broken up in 2003.

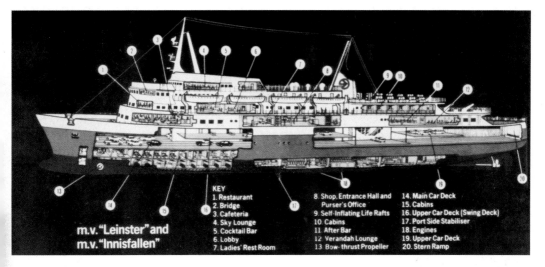

KEY

1. Restaurant	8. Shop, Entrance Hall and	14. Main Car Deck
2. Bridge	Purser's Office	15. Cabins
3. Cafeteria	9. Self-Inflating Life Rafts	16. Upper Car Deck (Swing Deck)
4. Sky Lounge	10. Cabins	17. Port Side Stabiliser
5. Cocktail Bar	11. After Bar	18. Engines
6. Lobby	12. Verandah Lounge	19. Upper Car Deck
7. Ladies' Rest Room	13. Bow-thrust Propeller	20. Stern Ramp

m.v. "Leinster" and
m.v. "Innisfallen"

Above and below: Innisfallen was launched on 7 December 1968 at the yard of Werft Nobiskrug GmbH and entered service on the Swansea-Cork service. She was sold in 1980 and renamed *Corsica Viva*, then *Dominican Viva* in 1985, *Corsica Viva* in 1988, *Sardinia Viva* in 1992, *Caribia Viva* in 1993 and *Spirit of Independence* in 1994. In 1998 she became *Happy Dolphin*, then *Derin Deniz* in 2003. She was broken up Alang in 2004.

SAIL & RENT AND JETDRIVE TO IRELAND WITH B+I AND AVIS

From **£31.00** return per person.

B + I FERRY SERVICES 1981

Periods	LIVERPOOL TO DUBLIN			DUBLIN TO LIVERPOOL		
	Dep	Arr	Departure days	Dep	Arr	Departure days
1 Jan to 31 Dec	1200	1930	Thu & Fri*	1100	1800	Thu & Fri*
	2215	0700	Daily	2215	0700	Daily

Note: Between 19-22 Jan and 11-19 Feb the service will be subject to alteration. Please check at time of booking.   *Fri & Sat - 21 Jun to 5 Sep*

Periods	PEMBROKE TO CORK			CORK TO PEMBROKE		
	Dep	Arr	Departure days	Dep	Arr	Departure days
19 Jan to 22 Mar* 1 Apr to 24 May 11 Oct to 31 Dec	2200	0700	Sun, Tue, Thu	2200	0800	Mon, Wed, Fri
25 May to 11 Jul 13 Sep to 10 Oct	2200	0700	Sun Tue Thu Sat	0930	1730	Sun
				2200	0700	Mon, Wed, Fri
12 Jul to 12 Sep	2200	0700	Tue-Sun (incl)	0930	1730	Wed-Sun (incl.)
				2200	0700	Mon

Note: No sailings between 23-31 March.

Periods	PEMBROKE TO ROSSLARE			ROSSLARE TO PEMBROKE		
1 Jan to 31 Dec	0200	0600	Sun, Thu, Fri, Sat	0800	1200	Sun, Thu, Fri, Sat
	1345	1745	Daily	2030	0030	Daily

No Sailing Dec. 25 or 26.

B + I JETFOIL SERVICES 1981

Periods	LIVERPOOL TO DUBLIN			DUBLIN TO LIVERPOOL		
	Dep	Arr	Departure days	Dep	Arr	Departure days
8 May to 28 May	1600	1915	Mon-Fri (incl)	0745	1100	Sat
	1920	2235	Sat, Sun	1200	1515	Mon-Fri (incl)
				1500	1815	Sun
29 May to 18 Jul 30 Aug to 5 Oct	1600	1915	Mon-Thu (incl.)	1200	1515	Mon-Thu (incl)
	1145	1500	Fri & Sat	0745	1100	Fri & Sat
	1950	2305	Fri & Sat	1550	1905	Fri & Sat
	1920	2235	Sun	1500	1815	Sun
19 Jul to 29 Aug	1145	1500	Mon-Sat (incl)*	0745	1100	Mon-Sat (incl.)
	1950	2305	Mon-Sat (incl)	1550	1906	Mon-Sat
	1920	2235	Sun* see below	1500	1815	Sun*

Double sailings as Mon/Sat on Sundays Aug 2, 9 & 16.

Above, left and right: B&I operated a jetfoil service from Liverpool to Dublin. She was named *Cu na Mara* [Hound of the Sea] and was launched at Seattle in November 1979, arriving at Liverpool in February 1980 on board the *Antonia Johnson*. *Cu na Mara* sailed on her maiden voyage from Dublin on 25 April and the service was advertised as linking both city centres. The Mersey terminal was at the landing stage close to the ferries and at Dublin it was at Custom House Quay.

The 1981 season commenced on 8 May when the crossing time was reduced to three-and-a-quarter hours. However, there were mechanical problems during that season and an oil price increase and it was decided to finish the service and withdraw the vessel. *Cu na Mara* was laid up and eventually sold to operate a service in Japan on a shorter route and renamed *Ginga*.

Above and right: The Atlantic Steam Navigation Company operated a roll-on/roll-off ferry service from Preston to Larne in Northern Ireland. In 1957/8 two new purpose-built vessels entered service and were named *Ionic Ferry* and *Bardic Ferry*. *Bardic Ferry* sailed on her maiden voyage on 2 September 1957 and *Ionic Ferry* on 10 October the following year. However, in the early 1970s they were forced to withdraw their services from Preston because of tidal restrictions and instead transferred to Cairnryan on Loch Ryan. They also operated a service from Felixstowe to Holland and both routes were sold to Townsend Thoresen.

Ionic Ferry (above) became *Kamasin* in 1976, *Tamerlane* in 1980 and was broken up at Aliaga in 1988. *Bardic Ferry* (below) was sold in 1976 becoming *Nasim II* and was also broken up at Aliaga in 1988.

NOTICE TO MARINERS.

No. 12 — 1962.

LIVERPOOL BAY
HOVERCRAFT

A Hovercraft passenger service is expected to be in operation between Wallasey and Rhyl starting 20th July and lasting for about four months. The service will only operate during daylight hours.

Preliminary operations of the Hovercraft are expected to commence on 14th July, 1962.

The Hovercraft operators have agreed that when at sea the Hovercraft shall observe the International Regulations for Preventing Collisions at Sea with the following modifications:—

(1) Since the Hovercraft is capable of high speed and can operate over shallow waters and sandbanks she will have particular regard to Rule 27 and in the circumstances in which under Rules 19 and 21 she is in the position of a stand-on ship she will consider herself to be in the position of a give-way ship and will keep well clear of ships.

(2) Owing to the noise of operation of the Hovercraft she will make no sound signals and she will not be able to hear sound signals made by ships.

The landing area at Wallasey will be adjacent to the disused Leasowe Lighthouse (52° 25'N, 3° 7'W) and at Rhyl will be on the foreshore, approx. 53° 19'N, 3° 30'W.

The Hovercraft, when approaching or leaving a terminal will steer a course approximately at right angles to the coast for about ½ mile.

A large red square flag will be flown from a flag staff at each of the terminals when Hovercraft are arriving or departing.

This page: In 1962 an experimental hovercraft service was operated between Wallasey and Rhyl in North Wales. The service was inaugurated on 20 July by a British Midland hovercraft.

Above and right: Terrier Link Lines [Coast Lines Group] (1957, 1098grt, 67 x 11m, 11kt)
She was built as *Ebba Robbert* and became *Sterge* in 1959 and *Terrier* in 1963. Renamed *Murrell* in 1972, *Quijote* in 1974 and *Omar G* in 1996.

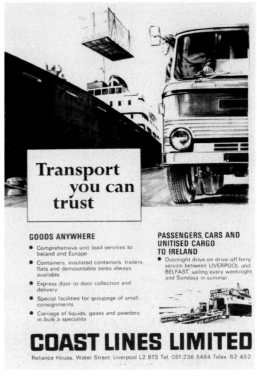

Transport
you can
trust

GOODS ANYWHERE

● Comprehensive unit load services to Ireland and Europe

● Containers, insulated containers, trailers, flats and demountable tanks always available

● Express door-to-door collection and delivery

● Special facilities for groupage of small consignments

● Carriage of liquids, gases and powders in bulk a speciality

PASSENGERS, CARS AND UNITISED CARGO TO IRELAND

● Overnight drive-on drive-off ferry service between LIVERPOOL and BELFAST, sailing every weeknight and Sundays in summer

COAST LINES LIMITED
Reliance House, Water Street, Liverpool L2 8TS Tel: 051-236 5464 Telex 62 452

Bison Link Lines (1961, 2,163grt, 79 x 13m, 12kt)
She became *Norbank* in 1972 and *Flamingo* in 1979 and was broken up in 1990.

Caledonian Coast Coast Lines (1948, 1,265grt, 84 x 12m, 14kt)
She was built for the Aberdeen Steam Navigation Co. Ltd for the London to Liverpol passenger route. In 1967 she was chartered by the Brocklebank Line and renamed *Makalla*, becoming *Ahmadi Coast* in 1968 and was broken up at Cartagena in 1974.

Cheshire Coast (1954, 1,202grt) and *Wirral Coast* (1962, 881grt).
Cheshire Coast was chartered to the Brocklebank Line in 1967 and renamed *Malabar*, becoming *Spartan Prince* in 1967 on charter to Prince Line, then *Cheshire Coast* and *Venture* in 1971, *Azelia* in 1974 and was broken up at Cartagena in 1980. *Wirral Coast* was built by Cammell Laird at Birkenhead and was renamed *Shevrell* in 1972, *Portmarnock* in 1974, *Nadia I* in 1979 and sank at Khalde in November, 1985.

Cambrian Coast Coast Lines (1958, 560grt, 57 x 9m, 10kt)
She was launched as *Jan T* and was sold in 1971 becoming *Lorraine Din*, *Zircon* in 1981, *Glenhaven* in 1982, and was broken up at Milford Haven in 1988.

Kilkenny B&I Line (1937, 1,320grt, 84 x 12m, 12kt)
She became *Cork* in 1971 and was sold for breaking up in 1974 at Dalmuir after a serious mechanical failure.

Kingsnorth Fisher James Fisher & Sons (1966, 2,480grt, 84m x 17m, 12kt)
She was renamed *New Generation* in 1990, *New Gen* in 2001 and broken up at Alang later that year.

Valzell J. Tyrrell Ltd (1935, 576grt, 54 x 9m, 8kt)
She was built as *Arbroath*, becoming *Valzell* in 1963 and was broken up at Cork in 1972.

Staley Bridge John Summers & Sons Ltd (1940, 297grt, 42 x 8m, 10kt)
She was broken up at Bow Creek in 1991.

Above: The Lady Grania Arthur Guinness & Co. (1952, 1,151grt, 65 x 11m, 11kt)
She became *The Lady Scotia* in 1978 and was lost off the Baja peninsular in 1981.

Left: Mountstewart Belfast, Mersey & Manchester S.S. Co. (1955, 906grt, 69 x 11m, 11kt)
She was built as *Essex Coast* becoming *Mountstewart* in 1957. Sold in 1968 and renamed *Evdelos Michalis* in 1972, *Proodos* in 1976, *Manuel* in 1979 and was broken up at Salamina in 1986.

Right: Farringay J.H.Griffin (1944, 461grt, 45 x 8m)

Built as *Empire Farringay* becoming *Farringay* in 1946, *Claire* in 1979 and broken up at Corunna in 1981.

Below: Vacuum Pioneer Vacuum Oil Co. Ltd (1953, 1,650grt, 80 x 12m, 11kt)

Collided with *Worthing* (1957, 1,873grt) off Haisborough on 13 October 1970 and arrived at Hughes Bolckow in Blyth for demolition on 24 October.

Alexandra tug *Wellington* (1926, 285grt).

Lamey, Rea, Alexandra and Liverpool Screw Lighterage tugs gather in Langton lock to prepare for their towage duties for the day.

Foylemore Johnson, Warren Lines Ltd (1958, 208grt)
She was renamed *St. Budoc* in 1983.

J.H. Lamey (1963, 200grt) and *William Lamey* (1959, 166grt) prepare to dock at Alfred Lock, Birkenhead after completing their towage duties for the day. *J.H.Lamey* was renamed *Hornby* in 1970. *William Lamey* was renamed *Wapping* in 1970, *Theodoros I* in 1985 and *Agios Rafail* in 2002 and *Fox I* in 2004.

Game Cock V North West Tugs Ltd (1953, 218grt)
She was sold to Greek interests in 1971 becoming *Vernicos Costas* and was broken up in 1989.

North Cock North West Tugs Ltd (1936, 201grt)
She was renamed *Hornby* in 1967.

Anita Lamey J.H. Lamey, Ltd (1920, 220grt)
She was built as *Thunderer*, becoming *Anita Lamey* in 1953.

James Lamey J.H. Lamey, Ltd (1928, 260grt)
She was built as *Flying Eagle* and became *James Lamey* in 1959, *Lilias* in 1966 and was broken up by Haulbowline Industries at Cork in 1970.

Egerton Alexandra Towing Co. Ltd (1965, 142grt) Sold in 1992 becoming *Caribe I* owned by the Oil Transport Company, Dominican Republic.

Above: *Canada* Alexandra Towing Co. Ltd (1951, 237grt)
She was sold in 1969 to Italian owners and was renamed *Strepitoso* and was broken up in 1988 at Brindisi.

Below: *Huskisson* Alexandra Towing Co. Ltd (1934, 201grt)
Broken up in 1965.

North Buoy (1959, 219grt) and *Canning* (1954, 200grt) assist the Scindia vessel *Jalaganga* (1958, 8,058grt) to berth in Canada Dock, Liverpool. *North Buoy* became *Caraggioso* in 1973 and was broken up in 1988 at Brindisi.

Alexandra tugs prepare to leave Gladstone lock.

Maplegarth (1961, 230grt) prepares to berth at Princess Landing stage in 1965.
She became *Seagarth* in 1992.

Rea and Lamey tugs entering Gladstone lock.

Applegarth Rea Towing (1951, 231grt)

On 13 January 1960 she was assisting *Perthshire* into Birkenhead Docks and sank off Woodside Stage, after colliding with the vessel. Only one of her crew of six were saved by the tug *Throstlegarth* and she was raised, re-fitted and returned to service the following year. She continued to work on the Mersey for another ten years and was sold to the Holyhead Towing Company in 1971 becoming *Afon Cefni*. In 1973 was renamed *Achilles* when sold to Greek interests, *Vernicos Christina* in 1975 and was broken up in Perama in 1980.

Opposite above: Kerne Liverpool Lighterage Co. Ltd (1913, 63grt)

Opposite below: Mersey No. 26 Mersey Docks & Harbour Board (1948, 70 x 12m)

She was built at Port Glasgow by Ferguson Bothers and was sold the Greek interests in 1971 and renamed *Triaena*, she was then sold for breaking up and arrived at San Esterban on 13 April 1974 in tow from Liverpool.

Mersey No.27 Mersey Docks & Harbour Board (1949, 1,363grt, 70 x 12m)
She was a Grab Hopper Dredger built by Ferguson Brothers at Port Glasgow and was also sold to
Spanish Shipbreakers at San Sebastian de Pravia where she arrived on 13 April 1974.

H.M. Denham Mersey Docks & Harbour Board (1981, 16 x 7m)
Built by McTay Marine at Bromborough, Wirral, as a catamaran survey vessel. She sank in East
Brocklebank Dock and was raised and repaired and is now owned by Denham Charters, Liverpool.

Birket Mersey Docks & Harbour Board (1942, 53 x 17m)
She was built in Paisley by Fleming & Ferguson and was purchased by the M. D. & H. B. from the
Government in 1946. She was sold to British Transport Docks, Hull in 1979.

Salvor Mersey Docks & Harbour Board (1947, 50 x 11m)

Built by Ferguson Brothers Limited at Port Glasgow as a salvage vessel, she was sold to Pemberton & Carlyon (Shipbreakers) Ltd and towed from Liverpool to Garston on 29 November 1978 to be broken up. Her mast and derricks are now positioned on the traffic island at Liverpool Pier Head.

Vigilant Mersey Docks & Harbour Board (1953, 50 x 11m)
Built by J.Thornycroft at Southampton as a salvage vessel. She was renamed *Staunch* in 1978 and broken up at Garston that year.

Aestus Mersey Docks & Harbour Board (1949, 23 x 6m)
Built by W.J. Yarwood at Northwich, Cheshire, as a survey vessel. She was sold to P.J. Penny, Hydro Surveyor, in 1981 and to Acecape Marine Ltd. the following year. Purchased by Tamahine Shipping in 1985 and H. Stewart Bracket (Metals) Ltd, she was broken up at Birkenhead in 1999.

Edmund Garner Mersey Docks & Harbour Board (1953, 52 x 10m)
A pilot boat built by Philip & Son Ltd at Dartmouth, she was acquired by the Merseyside Maritime Museum in 1971 as an exhibit and is open to the public at Albert Dock, Liverpool.